Clarence Gohdes is James B. Duke Professor Emeritus of American Literature, Duke University. He has published widely in the field of American literature, has edited *Hunting in the Old South*, and during his more than fifty years in Durham, North Carolina, has become a gifted gardener and a student of North Carolina wines.

Scuppernong

Overleaf: The Scuppernong Grape (*from* American Agriculturist, *XXVII [November, 1868], 413*)

CLARENCE GOHDES

Scuppernong

NORTH CAROLINA'S GRAPE

AND ITS WINES

1982

Duke University Press

Durham, N.C.

© 1982, Duke University Press

Library of Congress Cataloging in Publication Data

Gohdes, Clarence Louis Frank, 1901–
  Scuppernong: North Carolina's grape and its wines.

  Includes bibliographical references and index.
  1. Muscadine grape—North Carolina—History.
2. Viticulture—North Carolina—History.   3. Wine and
wine making—North Carolina—History.   I. Title.
SB387.76.N67G63   634'.83   81–9873
ISBN 0–8223–0460–0   AACR2

Printed in the United States of America

To Michael Baten and Neil Kaminsky

Contents

List of Illustrations

Preface

The nation's oldest native wine grape of continuing importance was named *scuppernong* in 1811, shortly after a North Carolina census taker reported that growers of the fruit in an area near a river by that name were engaged in a wine business extensive enough to qualify as a new American industry. The grape is a sport of the wild muscadine (*Vitis rotundifolia*), native only to the southern states. Its original discoverer among European explorers or settlers is unknown, though folklore has it that Sir Walter Raleigh's Lost Colony savored its delicious flavor and a specimen extant on Roanoke Island is falsely advertised as the "mother vine." A flurry of interest following the census taker's announcement led to a lively spread of grape planting so that by 1840 North Carolina was ranked the number-one wine producer of the Union, a distinction then of small economic concern and one soon lost to Georgia or other states. While a few commercial wineries from time to time were started up here and there, the manufacture of scuppernong wine was largely a home industry. However, wine pressed from the muscadines by commercial vintners occasionally won awards in Vienna and Paris, and in 1904 a bottle of sparkling scuppernong made by a Carolina firm captured the prestigious blue ribbon for champagnes in the international competition held in connection with the Louisiana Purchase Exposition in St. Louis. The winner was Paul Garrett, who started his notable career as America's chief vintner in Halifax County, North Carolina, and eventually reaped a huge fortune from a veritable grape empire extending from coast to coast. Garrett made the scuppernong the most popular wine of the United States in the years just prior to the advent of national Prohibition under the name Virginia Dare, which he chose for his most salable brand. At the outset it was made wholly of the southern *rotundifolia*, but as supplies of the grape ran short of the demand Virginia Dare was blended with larger and larger infusions of New York or California wines, the muscadine ultimately providing merely flavor and bouquet.

It is the intention of the author of this book to set forth the main outlines of the history of the scuppernong with special reference to its

North Carolina connections and also to provide illustrations of other aspects of Tarheel wines and vines. The activities of Garrett and Company in exploiting the grape are of course essential to the story and naturally move the setting beyond the borders of the South. The book ends with a brief treatment of the repercussions of the current wine boom in North Carolina following the General Assembly's belated effort to promote its most celebrated native fruit.

In gathering information for the present study I have gone to the sources, primarily the manuscripts, periodicals, and books in the Flowers Collection of Duke University's Perkins Library and to the North Carolina Historical Collection housed in the Library of the University of North Carolina in Chapel Hill. I have thus retraced the steps of F. C. Reimer, a professional horticulturist who led the way in the scientific study of the scuppernong and its annals. All authentic accounts of the origins of the grape confirm his version of the early story of the muscadine. Of these accounts the most important is the section on North Carolina in *The Wines of America*, a prodigious but fascinating survey written by Leon D. Adams, originally published in Boston in 1973 and revised in a second edition issued in New York five years later. I have been enlightened considerably by Mr. Adams's vast store of information on the American wine scene since the 1930s. I have also used with profit Professors Maynard A. Amerine and Vernon L. Singleton's volume called *Wine: An Introduction*, published by the University of California Press and revised in a second edition, 1977.

It is a pleasure to record my thanks to the many individuals who have provided, or opened the doors to, information upon which the present volume depends. Beginning with my own colleagues at Duke University, I mention particularly John Alden, Carl Anderson, the late Jay B. Hubbell, Joseph J. Spengler, Craufurd Goodwin, Paul Kramer, and Aubrey Naylor. Mattie Russell and W. R. Erwin of the Library's Manuscript Department have been uniformly kind and helpful, as have also G. S. T. Cavanagh of the Medical Center's historical library and the Perkins Reference Department's experts Joseph Rees, David Wells, Jane Vogel, and Mary Canada. Frank L. Williams at Edenton and Ann Fussell at Rose Hill have added to my knowledge of the wineries with which they have been associated, and Fred Cumbo, James Weaver, and Ed. Estes of North Carolina State University in Raleigh have likewise answered my queries. Similarly, I am obliged to Thornton M. Mitchell, State Archivist, and to Jeffrey J. Crow, head of the General Publications Branch of the Historical

Publications Section of the Carolina Department of Cultural Resources. Sarah Lemmon of Meredith College and Elizabeth Moore of Edenton have shared their knowledge of local history with me, and Mrs. Chase C. Padgett of the Home Economics Extension Service has gone out of her way to fill in gaps in my knowledge, as has also William S. Powell, chief authority on North Carolina history. Likewise J. W. McGwigan of Enfield and his niece Louise M. Hall of Chapel Hill have put me in their debt, as have also Martha Holloman of the Halifax County Library and Maurice E. Taylor of the Wilmington Public Library. Dorothy Roberts and Doris C. Ralston have kindly helped with typing, and Myrna Jackson with the editing.

Other than North Carolinians, I wish to mention here the following: John C. Broderick and Helen F. Ulibarre of the Library of Congress, J. O. Eidson, his wife Perrin, and R. P. Lane of the University of Georgia, Morris Cox of Clemson University, John A. Mortensen of the University of Florida, John A. Lipe and Jerome A. Loving of Texas A. and M., J. P. Overcash of Mississippi State University, Blair Rouse and J. H. Moore of the University of Arkansas, G. D. Oberle, now retired in Geneva, New York, and Vincent P. Carosso of New York University, David W. Cain of Fresno, California, Joan V. Ingalls, librarian of the Wine Institute in San Francisco, Leon D. Adams, the chief historian of American wines, and Mrs. Rexford Tugwell, Louise Gohdes, Sue Winkler, and Robert Walker, all Californians. Finally, I wish to thank Mrs. L. J. Barden of Rochester, New York, especially for providing me with a copy of the dictated early reminiscences of her father, Paul Garrett, whose career and the history of the scuppernong grape may be said to have been intertwined, if not interfused, for so many decades.

January, 1981

Scuppernong

CHAPTER I

The Early History of the Grape

Of the bounteous store of natural gifts that have rolled from the Horn of Plenty upon the soil of North Carolina few have been more celebrated than the scuppernong grape. It is a sport of the species *Vitis rotundifolia*, commonly called muscadine, which is native to the southern states and grows nowhere else save as an exotic. The muscadine, it is no exaggeration to say, could well be substituted for cotton in the first line of "Dixie" if one were to bow to botanical realism. The scuppernong variety of muscadine has a tough skin and is bronzy green in color, rather than black or purplish as were its ancestors. Its size, to use traditional Tarheel parlance, is "about that of a hog's eye." As is the case with all muscadines, the fruit does not grow in conventional bunches, and when ripe it can be readily shaken from its vine. Its abundant juice is so deliciously sweet, with a kind of musky, fruity flavor, that when its unusual color attracted attention, in the general vicinity of present-day Columbia, N.C., possibly toward the end of the eighteenth century, specimens were transplanted or seeds or cuttings sown on neighboring farms and gardens whence in time its reputation spread throughout the botanical world. Of the score or so of grape species native to the United States it was the earliest to prove of an interest to wine makers that continues down to the present day.

At first it was simply called the Big White Grape, for the name *scuppernong*, as we shall see, was not applied to it until some time after its choice qualities and immense productiveness were known in the tidewater region of North Carolina. It came to particular notice in Tyrrell County, along the banks of a short stream that broadens into an arm of Albemarle Sound and had long since been named the Scuppernong. There is also, toward the head of that river, a body of inland water, surprisingly clear, which was also called Scuppernong Lake, though its official name is Phelps, after one of the two local hunters who penetrated the dense thickets surrounding it and "discovered" it in 1755. Shortly before he fired the first shot at Fort Sumter, Edmund Ruffin inspected the vicinity and declared that "no equal space of territory in all the States . . . has been so little visited or seen by other than its residents."[1]*

In addition to a river and a lake, also called Scuppernong were various settlements near them, though the spellings that crop up in old records leave something to be desired. An example is provided by John Urmston, an Anglican missionary, who in 1711 reported "forty or fifty families" then resident at "Allegator and Scogalong."[2] Those communities, however, appear to have been too remote for visitation then, probably all to the good of the reputation of their inhabitants, for such parishioners as Urmston had seen he dubbed "a nest of the most notorious profligates upon earth." His vestrymen irked him by bringing their rum bottles to sessions; and, as for the whole lot of these Carolinians, he concluded, they "think there is no difference between a Gentleman and a labourer: all are fellows at Foot Ball."[3] In 1740 a governmental warehouse was ordered built along the Scuppernong River, but no town was authorized until 1787, when a member of the Spruill family presented a petition for one at a place called Back Landing. About the same time, Josiah Collins, Nathaniel Allen, and Samuel Dickinson were granted a right-of-way for constructing a canal between the river and the lake.[4] The affluent Collins family, soon joined by that of Charles Pettigrew, were the first to make the upper Scuppernong River settlements the domain of rich gentlemen. Aided by platoons of slaves, more than three hundred of them freshly imported from Africa, they drained the fields and established plantations where rice and, later, corn and wheat were successfully grown.[5]

The word *scuppernong* is derived from *askúponong*, which being interpreted from the Southern Algonquian language, means "at (or in) the place (country) of the *āskúpo*," the *āskúpo* in turn being "the Magnolia glauca, a small tree growing in swamps (or 'bays' as magnolia swamps are called in North Carolina)."[6] This plant, now popularly known as "sweet bay, swamp bay, swamp sassafras, bay laurel, etc.," was mentioned as early as 1588 by Thomas Hariot: "Ascopo a kind of tree very like unto Lawrell, the bark is hoat and spicie."[7] Numerous subsequent travel-book writers similarly mention it, for example an Irish physician John Brickell, who lived for a time at Edenton and in 1737 observed that the *ascopo* is a tree, so called by the Indians, "very like the *Laurel* in its leaves," though

---

*On an earlier visit, in 1839, Ruffin heard the story of the discovery of Lake Phelps and related it in his *Farmers' Register* (VII [1839], 703). He noted also, on the way from Plymouth, "the Scuppernong grape vines, trained in the manner used in that part of the country, and on Roanoke Island."

he confessed he had never seen it growing. An Indian, however, procured a branch of it for his inspection and assured him that it was "plentifully to be met with" at riverheads and near the mountains.[8]

Brickell also recorded: "There are but few *Vineyards* planted in this Colony at present, for I have seen but one small one at Bath-Town and another at *Neus* [New Bern], of the White Grape, the same with the Madera. I have drank the Wine it produced, which was exceeding good." He added that the colonists had planted slips of various "curious Vines" which, given time, he opined, would make good wine, "there being nothing wanting but industry."[9] It may be argued that Brickell knew our Big White Grape, but the same might be said of John Lawson, Captain John Smith of Pocahontas fame, and of sundry others.[*]

No records coming from the late eighteenth century suggest that the "country" grape was then celebrated even near the lake or along the river or at any of the settlements or landings named Scuppernong. When in 1773 Josiah Quincy, a gentleman-patriot with an eye and taste for wines, toured the chief seaboard towns from Charleston, Brunswick, Wilmington, New Bern, Bath, and Edenton, on into Virginia, he noticed that the gentry, who entertained him quite royally, drank claret and port in preference to Madeira or Lisbon and that the Allstons on their estate (present-day Brook Green Gardens, S.C.) had propagated "the Lisbon and Wine Island grapes with great success."[10]

And as for the humbler folk more typical of the "fellows at Foot Ball," in all probability Dr. Brickell's summary of their bibbing habits made in the 1730s still applied:

The Liquors that are common in *Carolina* at present and chiefly made use of, are, Rum, Brandy, Mault Drink; these they import. The following are made in the Country, *viz.* Cyder, Persimon-Beer, made of the fruit of that tree, Ceder Beer, made of Ceder-Berries; they also make beer of the green Stalks of Indian-corn, which they bruise and boyle. They likewise make Beer of Mollosses, or common Treacle, in the following manner, they take a gallon of Mollosses, a Peck of Wheaten Bran, a Pound of Hops, and a Barrel of Fountain Water, all which they boile together, and work up with yest, as we do our Malt Liquors; this is their common Small-Beer, and seems to me to be the pleasantest Drink, I ever tasted, either in the *Indies* or *Europe*, and I am satisfied more wholsom. This is made stronger in proportion, as People fancy.[11]

---

[*]Of the six kinds Lawson mentions, four he calls fox grapes. "The *Summer Fox-grapes* do not grow in clusters . . . and are as big as a large *Damson*. The Black sort are very common and plentiful all over this Province but the White are very scarce and seldom to be met with" (p. 108). Lawson had planted "some Grape-seed, which was of the *Jesuits* White Grape from *Madera*" (p. 119).

Doctor Brickell also remarked that both planters and Indians "indifferently used Castena or Yaupon, an *Indian Tea*."

In addition to the Scuppernong area, the White Grape was associated with another settlement not far removed, namely, Roanoke Island. Here so many vines were planted by the fishermen residents—and so many more visitors came than cut their way into the *ascopo* jungles—that the name *roanoke* was widely applied to the luscious muscadine, and the legend was—and still is—bruited about that Sir Walter Raleigh himself had the vines sought out and planted for the benefit of his colony there. And there are many who declare in unimpeachable sobriety that at least one vine still grows at Manteo to identify the mother of all the scuppernong progeny, even though often dubbed "The Sir Walter Raleigh Vine." Such yarns are, of course, without substantiation. Like the story of young Washington and the cherry tree, they are among the wild blue blunders of fancy. As for the antiquity of certain indubitably ancient scuppernong vines, we have, alas, no dendrochronological evidence. Most plants fabulous for purported antiquity have to be replaced from time to time, to satisfy the demands of the tourist trade. The romantic "old rose bush" of Hildesheim, Germany, and the rose on Edward Fitzgerald's grave at Boulge in England are prominent examples. And he would be a bold man indeed to declare before a congregation of grape growers that the vine in the grapery at Hampton Court near London provided dessert for Henry VIII.

For estimating the age of the vine admired by present-day visitors to Roanoke Island there is a bit of relevant information supplied in 1880 by John W. Evans, scion of a family long associated with storekeeping at Manteo. In that year William McMurtrie compiled an official *Report upon Statistics of Grape Culture and Wine Production in the U.S.*,[12] which ranked North Carolina second in the South in area planted, 2,639 acres, Carteret County leading with 500. Attached to the tables therein are excerpts from the letters of the several correspondents who supplied the basic data. Evans, who was one of these, is there quoted as follows: "There are two vines now living and bearing grapes on this Island that are from eighty to one hundred years old."[13] Is the now-living vine one of the two? There is further testimony. In 1909 a professional horticulturist, F. C. Reimer, published in Raleigh a pamphlet on *Scuppernong and Other Muscadine Grapes*[14] based on a pretty thorough investigation of the history as well as the characteristics of the *rotundifolia*. He had visited personally all the vines in the state that were then reported to be very old, found the most ancient to be in Tyrrell County, and reported for Roanoke Island "five vines of about equal age . . . in two straight rows" [15]—sure evidence that they were survivors of a modern vineyard. Reimer also concluded that when a muscadine enters into its senior stage its trunk is not a single stem but more nearly resembles a bundle of stems. The earliest vineyard of commercial consequence known to have been planted on Roanoke Island dates from about 1859.*

One cannot be sure of the age of the matriarchal vine still growing at Manteo in the 1980s, but one can be certain that its motherhood is the product of folklore stimulated by advertising. "Mother Vineyard" is the trademark of a winery which in 1956 was transferred from Roanoke Island to Petersburg, Virginia. [16] There its labels continued for a time to indulge in fanciful history involving Sir Walter as they adhered to bottles of sweet scuppernong. The grapes, the labels also once stated, were grown in North Carolina.

Undismayed by failure to connect the Big White Grape, alias scuppernong, alias roanoke, with the Lost Colony, one must admit that the island was a favored site for growing the juicy muscadine. There were many like Lemuel Sawyer, who recalled for the readers of the U.S. Patent Office Report for 1849[17] that, as early as 1815, he had sailed from his home in Washington, N.C., with his slaves and his press and his barrels, to squeeze the grapes on Roanoke Island.† And James G. Hall, of Currituck, in 1827 stated in a letter to the Baltimore-based *American Farmer* that the White Grape was "a native of the northeastern part of North Carolina," and grew "spontaneously on Roanoke Island and its vicinity, and formerly was universally termed the Roanoke grape." But, "as its excellence as a wine grape was first tested at Scuppernong, the grape has improperly obtained that name abroad." [18] He guessed that the span of life for the variety would be "fifty or sixty years," but with proper care it would survive longer. And in conclusion he opined that only a few years earlier little attention had been paid to the grape but at the moment it was rising fast in "importance."

Of the rising importance there can be no question, for in 1830 William Prince, of a celebrated family of nurserymen located at Flushing, N.Y.,

---

*F. S. Proctor of Edenton started a vineyard and winery there, with scuppernongs, Concords, Isabellas, etc. "Now has 3000 vines there in a flourishing condition," "a new experiment for this section of the country" (*North Carolina Planter*, II [June, 1859], 190).

†Sawyer stated that the farmers on the banks of the Scuppernong River made grapes their principal crop, which they bartered for corn and flour, since their light, sandy soil prevented ordinary farming.

in his *Treatise on the Vine* not only repeated much from "the most perfect account" of the grape, as he termed Hall's screed, but added the "opinion of many intelligent persons that the Scuppernong, or Roanoke wine" had "a richness and a peculiarly fine flavour" unknown in the foreign wines that reached America. "All its advantages considered, it promises, at no distant day, to form the basis of innumerable vineyards in different sections of the country," he prophesied.[19] Certainly the name *scuppernong* was taking on, for Prince set a seal of approval on the confusion that then existed—and still exists—over the use of the name for the entire species of *Vitis rotundifolia* by speaking of green as well as white or black scuppernongs—and even reported a Virginian as having informed him of a red one. These may all have been seedlings of the genuine scuppernong.

To add to the taxonomic confusion, still another name for the Big White Grape emerged in the publicity emanating from the 1820s. An unidentified correspondent, writing from New Bern in March, 1827, described for the *Farmer* his twelve-year-old vine, which covered fifty square feet of scaffolding and produced "sixty gallons and upward" of wine. And the name of this prodigy, he declared, was not scuppernong but Hickman.[20] Shortly afterward, another New Bern gentleman, signing himself merely "A North Carolinian," firmly insisted that no one in his neighborhood had ever known the grape until it was brought there by "one Hickman, whose name it bears."[21] And William Blackledge, in recommending the introduction of the scuppernong—of which he had known for forty years—into South Carolina and Georgia, likewise stated its name in the New Bern area to be Hickman.[22] Along the Cape Fear River, where it was being planted in increasing numbers, the grape was also called Hickman before the battle over nomenclature was lost. Just who this hero was is unknown, though Judge Gaston, author of "The Old North State Forever," claimed Hickman as a neighbor who was said to have brought the plant from Tyrrell County in 1760.[23] As editors and correspondents added to the discussions in North Carolina, and news came in from other southern states of the fabulous harvests and ease in cultivating the scuppernong, questions were raised as to who was the first to assign its name. Who named the baby? At the time, and ever since, frequent reference was made to a letter written in Raleigh on June 17, 1817, by Dr. Calvin Jones and addressed to Hutchins G. Burton of Halifax (who later served in Congress, 1819–24, and thereafter as governor).[24] This epistle, first printed, with some trimming, in the *American Farmer* for January 11, 1822,[25] was obviously calculated to inform the recipient of the chief facts bearing on scuppernong wine. The name, Jones stated, first appeared in a weekly newspaper, the *Star*, founded in Raleigh and edited by himself in conjunction with Thomas Henderson, Jr. It was applied by the editors to both the grape and the wine "in compliment to James Blount, of Scuppernong, who first diffused a general knowledge of it in several well written communications in our paper"—and, he added, "it is cultivated with more success on that river than in any other part of the state, perhaps, except the Island of Roanoke." He had recently visited that island, he went on, and after describing the scaffold supports for the vines, explained that a fifth or sixth part of "proof spirit" was added in making the wine. He had also of late attended a party in Raleigh where he had sampled a bottle of it, "made by Mr. Pettigrew at Phelps Lake," which he pronounced "light, clear and pleasant." He had been told that it resembled the Constantia wine from the Cape of Good Hope,* and he himself judged it to be "not inferior to Teneriffe," a then common type of Canary. In Raleigh, he apologized, "we have had much of the Scuppernong wine . . . but few fair samples," for the reputation "suddenly attained here in consequence of our newspaper publications occasioned a great deal to be manufactured of honey and other ingredients." He had heard that French brandy was the best spirit to add. And he asked Burton whether the tramping around on the ground near the vines such as he had observed at Roanoke Island was "advantageous" to the plants.

This query suggests that Dr. Jones may have been innocent of knowledge with respect to the details of viticulture, but surely he had had a bit of brushing up on his wines. Of his veracity there can be no doubt. Before presenting the confirmatory details, it may be well to explain who he was. Massachusetts-born, trained as a physician, author of a treatise on scarlet fever published at Catskill, N.Y., in 1794, Jones came to North Carolina for reasons unknown, organized the first medical society in the state as well as the Wake Troop of cavalry, in 1806, eventually rose in the militia to major-general in charge of coastal defense during the War of 1812, was Grand Master of North Carolina Masons, served for a generation on the board of trustees of the University in Chapel Hill, to which he gave a collection for a museum, and just prior to moving in 1832 to

---

* "This Cape grape appears to have been really an offshoot of the wild fox-grape, or *Vitis labrusca*, and it is, therefore, the forerunner of the varieties [*e.g.* Catawba, Concord] which we now cultivate everywhere in our vineyards. It was also known as the Schuylkill Muscadel and Clifton's Constantia" (L. H. Bailey, *Sketch of the Evolution of Our Native Fruits*, 2d ed. [New York, 1906], p. 43). The grape was also called the Alexander, after a gardener by that name who found it growing near the Schuylkill River. It produced the only wine made from native grapes that had any vogue of consequence prior to that of the scuppernong.

Tennessee, sold his six-hundred-acre farm at Wake Forest to the protocollege then called the Baptist Literary Institute, designed to train young ministers and youth in general "to knowledge of science and agriculture." He also served as the first postmaster of Wake Forest.

Truly a Renaissance man in the Old North State, Calvin Jones (1775–1846) was also a prolific writer on agricultural subjects.[26] When British officials put out a lengthy questionnaire on economic and related subjects in 1828, he took on the task of answering on behalf of his neighborhood some of the 106 questions entailed. One of them, by the way, had been formulated "by the celebrated Mr. Malthus," who was then accumulating data for his population studies. Particularly interesting are Jones's statements with respect to livestock and to slavery. He mentions horses roaming wild east of Raleigh and the sale of Negro boys in that city "before the War": "as we then reckoned Virginia money, the rule was, pound for pound."[27]

An examination of Jones's newspaper, the Raleigh *Star*, fully confirms the claims made in his letter to Burton. The first relevant item, in the issue for December 21, 1809, sounds like a hasty summary of exciting news recently acquired—and, in fact, that is exactly what it is. The item is headed in italics: *"Description of an extraordinary and excellent kind of grape, produced in the north-eastern part of North Carolina, but not generally known even in that state."* After mentioning the size, color, and taste of the grape, the article states that it had been cultivated for "a number of years" in the vicinity of Lake Phelps but it was "not clearly understood whence it originated." Few "old settlers about the lake," it further noted, but what had a vine planted at the base of a tree or trailing on scaffolding made of poles lying on forked posts, and "many people" owned vines that without any pruning yielded a barrel of wine each. The local process of winemaking is then briefly outlined (one part of brandy to three of juice), but the hope is entertained that better methods may be discovered, especially since "there are several gentlemen of information sending to the people in that neighborhood to make wine for them." The item ends: "Some have tried fermentation but it did not answer."*

From time to time the *Star* printed letters from Joseph Cooper, an ardent champion of native grapes, who offered encouragement and instruction in the art of winemaking from his experimental farm at Cooper's Point, New Jersey.[28] Cooper is now honored as "the first man in America

---

*The Scuppernong River product appears to have been the forerunner of the California Angelica.

to undertake as his life's work the breeding of plants."[29] But the most important communication came from James Blount, who had been gathering information as the U.S. Census reporter for Washington County. At that time the census was in the hands of U.S. marshals, and Blount's information was first transmitted to Beverly Daniel, in Raleigh, marshal of the North Carolina district, who, it seems, passed the news on to the governor, Benjamin Smith, and to Jones.

When the *Star*, on January 31, 1811, printed the news that during the previous season 1368 gallons of wine had been manufactured in a county which returned "only 384 militia," enquiries about this "interesting branch of our Infant Manufactures" came so thick and fast that Blount was asked for further details. The large white grape from which "the most of the wine" was made, he explained, was thought to be a native, and he, himself, had seen just such a vine in the woods some three years earlier. If grown from seed, he was informed, the vines would produce purple grapes larger than those obtained from vines matured from cuttings, and if properly pruned and fertilized one single plant would be worth fifty apple trees, for it might yield fifty to a hundred bushels of grapes. Blount forwarded a parcel of seeds from the vines at Scuppernong, "where the greatest quantity of the finest grapes are to be found," and asked the marshal to turn some of them over to the editors of the *Star*, to whom he promised a later explanation of the prevailing methods employed by the newly discovered vignerons.

Jones acknowledged receipt of the seeds from Major Daniel and added that some of them had already been shipped off to "friends and acquaintances," among whom were "Dr. Barton, Professor of Botany in Philadelphia, and Mr. Joseph Cooper, an eminent agriculturalist in New Jersey, and also Dr. Hosack, proprietor of the Botanic Garden in New-York." The choice of these men now seems amazingly precocious, for Benjamin S. Barton, physician and naturalist, looms large in history as the first American to write a general book on botany; Cooper, as we have seen, was one of the earliest predecessors of consequence to famed plant breeder Luther Burbank; and David Hosack was, like Barton, a distinguished professor of both medical and botanical subjects, whose Elgin Botanical Garden, on the present-day site of Rockefeller Center, is still honored in memory. Hosack was the physician who attended Alexander Hamilton at his duel with Aaron Burr.[30]

Jones further observed that the *Star* had earlier (Dec. 21, 1809) called attention to "this singular and excellent species of grapes which (for the sake of distinction, until we are better instructed) we shall denominate the *Scuppernong Grape*." Thus the name was given—in a subordinate clause. On March 7, 1811, however, the *Star* put a clincher on it by printing in large capitals THE SCUPPERNONG GRAPE. Under this heading notice was given that Dr. James Mease of Philadelphia had seen Blount's account of the new grape and had requested "some specimens of the vine and branches" for use in a "Natural History of the Vines of the United States," which he planned to publish with colored engravings.[31] Jones described how botanical specimens could be prepared, and directed readers to forward them to the Philadelphian via his paper or through the agency of "Alex Henderson at Newbern" or "Doctor de Rossett of Wilmington."* The choice of agents in the two port cities may be advanced as evidence that the presence of the Big White Grape in their neighborhoods was already recognized, but, more likely, the selection was governed merely by facility of transportation from those ports to Philadelphia.

The interest of Dr. Mease in the new grape may warrant a brief excursus, for it reveals a surprisingly quick response to the initial announcements in the *Star*. As secretary of the Pennsylvania Agricultural Society and member of the board of managers of the Company for the Improvement of the Vine he was, so to speak, at the main center of horticultural interest in the nation, and, like Joseph Cooper, was an ardent promoter of the cause of native American grapes. A wealthy physician, married to the daughter of Pierce Butler of South Carolina, he had his own private vineyard, consisting, it is said, of some three thousand vines.[32] He wrote extensively on medical topics, ranging from hydrophobia to the causes and cure of the sick headache, and published books on his natal Philadelphia and on natural history as well. He was on the qui vive, one might say, for native wine grapes, and in one of his books, *A Geological Account of the United States*, had ventured a brief prophecy that, with the help of European vintners, excellent wines would some day be produced to rival those from abroad.[33] And he had even indicated the best prospects at the time: a "little blue grape" from Pennsylvania (Alexander), the "bland" (Bland or Virginia Muscadel), "the grapes of the islands from Ohio," and the "bull" grape of South Carolina and Georgia (muscadine). News of the scuppernong from the swamps of North Carolina must have come to him as a delightful surprise.

At the end of his request for aid to Dr. Mease, Jones confided to the

*Henderson was probably a relative of Jones's partner in business. Armand J. De Rosset, of a prominent Cape Fear family, was port physician of Wilmington.

readers of the *Star* that since the publication of Blount's letter he had been told by "a Raleigh gentleman" that Sir Walter had carried back to England "a white grape that was esteemed among the best ever seen" in that country and "under the patronage of Queen Elizabeth it was extensively cultivated"—but, unfortunately, the "informant's memory did not serve him with the recollection of the source from which he derived his information." Thus it came to pass that folklore crept up on the Big White Grape as soon as it was named scuppernong.

Two weeks later another heading SCUPPERNONG GRAPE greeted the readers of the *Star* in introducing Blount's promised report on how the winemakers of Washington County handled the juice of their delicious grapes. Apparently, there was no standard method, he explained, but many of the vintners barreled it off immediately after using a cider press, adding one part of applejack to four of the juice. The "most approved method," however, was to let the must undergo fermentation and then draw it off into clean casks, three gallons of juice and one of brandy alternately, till the casks were filled. Formerly, Blount had learned, it was the practice to add honey, but some makers considered the grapes sufficiently sweet without any admixture.[34] One gathers from Blount's remarks that quite a few people had been making the wine for several years.

The paper followed this exposition with a short extract from a letter by "a friend in Philadelphia": "The cultivation of the grape in thy state has been a matter of surprise and interest; and if it should increase it may become of the first importance, not only as an article of commerce, but as a means of improving the morals of our country. That at first blush may appear strange. Yet I have not the smallest doubt but that the use of ardent Spirits . . . will decline just in proportion to the increase of wine. . . ." One may rest assured that the good friend did not know what the folks at Scuppernong were putting into their new wine. Nor did he know that the 1810 Census report of *Manufactures Within the State of North Carolina* indicated sixteen stills for Washington County, with an annual output of 3,631 gallons of whiskey or brandy—valued at a dollar a gallon, and for Tyrrell County 110 stills, with 4,000 gallons valued at $3500.[35] For the whole state 5,424 stills were reported as producing 1,386,691 gallons of whiskey and brandy, in value far outstripping tar, turpentine, etc. For the ordinary Tarheel a little wine was useful only for the bowels' sake—and the blackberries probably provided the best. But for day-in and day-out bibbing "hard licker" was standard. It was obtainable just about everywhere in the region.

Looking back over the initial publicity afforded the Big White Grape by the *Star*, one may conclude that there must have been special circumstances accounting for the rapid spread of the excitement of its discovery to the vinophiles of Philadelphia and the botanists of New York, as well as to Joseph Cooper in New Jersey. In a general way, interest had been stimulated all over the country in avoiding dependence on European products, as a result of the Embargo Act of 1807, subsequently followed by events culminating in the War of 1812. Though far from being a favorite American beverage, wine was nevertheless a standard article of transatlantic commerce. The advent of the scuppernong, thus, came at a propitious moment. Moreover, Calvin Jones seems to have had some special affiliation with the medical fraternity in New York and Philadelphia as well as with Joseph Cooper in New Jersey.

We may be sure that Benjamin Smith, elected governor of North Carolina in 1810, also had a hand in the matter. When it is remembered that seeds of the grape were sent to "Dr. Barton, Professor of Botany in Philadelphia" and that his full name was Benjamin Smith Barton, more than a casual connection may be imagined. But the governor's association with another grape is much clearer, for it was in his garden in Smithville (later to be called Southport) that Mrs. Isabella Gibbs secured a cutting from a vine destined in the years following 1816 to become a standard wine producer of New York, and named Isabella in her honor.[36] It is still grown in the Finger Lakes region of New York and elsewhere. For some time the Isabella was thought to be a North Carolina native. It is now considered a crossbreed, probably brought to the Wilmington area by Bernard Laspeyre, who claimed to have discovered it in a garden in Charleston, S.C.[37]

Another landed gentleman involved in the earliest publicity for the Carolina grape was Thomas Jefferson, the most knowledgeable of the Founding Fathers in the ways of vines and wines. While he once decided that it would take a long, long time for Americans to catch up with the hoary tradition of European vintners, and there were more important demands in the New World, he changed his mind radically, tried all manner of European as well as native varieties in his vineyard and, indeed, in 1773 joined with George Washington and others in abetting the settlement next to Monticello of Dr. Philip Mazzei and his group of Italians who undertook a business partnership to raise fruit and make wine.[38] Amid the distractions of war and public service he kept abreast of horticultural progress and after his return to Virginia experimented continually with new fruits and vegetables. When he learned of the scuppernong he tried to grow it but failed.

Jefferson, however, is more intimately associated with the history of the Carolina grape. It will be recalled that the most generally used document exploring the origin of the name was the letter written by Dr. Calvin Jones to H. G. Burton of Halifax, N.C., stating that the editors of the *Star* had named the new grape after Blount's account of it had appeared in their paper. This key document was dated June 17, 1817, but it was first published in the Baltimore *American Farmer* on January 11, 1822, over four years later. How did the editor of the *Farmer* acquire it? The answer is at hand in a note which Skinner printed in his magazine: "It was placed in our hands in the summer of 1820, by Mr. Jefferson, at whose table *Millet* was seen by us for the first time, in any shape."[39] Obviously, Burton had given Jones's explanatory letter to Jefferson, who in turn handed it on to Skinner, perhaps with the intention, certainly with the effect, of giving the grape further recognition. In the same year that Jones wrote to Burton, namely 1817, through his son-in-law J. W. Eppes, Jefferson had secured a barrel of the "Scuppernon," as he spelled it, with Burton acting as go-between in Washington County. On April 21, 1823, Francis Eppes wrote to his grandfather at Monticello:

I obtained from Col. Burton the address of several gentlemen who make the Carolina wine . . . persons in easy circumstances, who do not care to oblige, generally keeping the best for themselves. It was from Cox that your last and (I believe) my Fathers [*sic*] which you admired, were obtained. In case, however, that you might still prefer the wine makers themselves, he informed me that Ebinezer [*sic*] Pettigrew P.O. Edenton and George E. Spruel [Spruill] P.O. Plymouth make it best. The former will not always sell being very wealthy, the latter is not in as good circumstances, and owns the famous vine covering an acre of ground. Col. B. informed us that the vine does not grow from the slip, which accounts for the failure of yours.[40]

Instead of writing to Pettigrew or Spruill, whose names his grandson had obtained from Burton only after considerable coaxing, Jefferson chose to deal with Thomas Cox, a commission merchant of Plymouth, and on June 3, 1823, informed him that two casks of the wine received from him had been "really fine," but various other samples he had tasted from bottle or wood had been so adulterated as to make them "mere juleps." However, he put in an order for a thirty-gallon barrel, adding, politely, "under the absolute assurance that there shall be nothing in it but the pure juice of the grape"; if the wine soured, he promised, the risk would be his. In a postscript he asked Cox to tell him what was the proper age for ripening and drinking it.[41] Upon reviewing the foregoing information, one may be tempted to conclude that it was Jefferson who prompted Burton to find out how the promising new wine had obtained its name.

Although the gentry of the Scuppernong River area and Calvin Jones with his Raleigh *Star*, and the botanical doctors in Philadelphia provided impetus projecting the Big White Grape on the pathway to fame, John S. Skinner and his *American Farmer* did perhaps even more. His journal, a much more potent medium than a village newspaper, continually brought the grape to the attention of the "book-farmers" and nurserymen all along the eastern seaboard, and prospective vintners who planted the native grapes, usually after failing with the *vinifera* from abroad, were tempted to experiment with the newly heralded plant from North Carolina. When a grower sent him some grapes and a letter mentioning, among others, "the White Scuppernong," Skinner appended a note, "A large grape of delightful flavour" and headed the epistle: "With Specimens of Superb Grapes!!"[42] On another occasion he made room for a bit of "promotion" from Plymouth, N.C., dated April 10, 1825,[43] and signed by several men who asked to remain anonymous. Though much had been said "in private circles" of its merits, they observed, the scuppernong had not been introduced to "the view of the nation." Accordingly, they desired to point out, "several hundred casks" could readily be exported from Plymouth if sufficient encouragement were offered, and the local "wine manufacturers," a "population generally indigent," would at once rise into "comparative opulence" in the process. To quicken this social appeal, they announced that they were forwarding via Norfolk two dozen bottles, half of them to enable Skinner to judge the qualities of their vintage and the rest to display at the next Maryland "agricultural exhibition"—a fair, by the way, quite widely attended and highly regarded in the Baltimore area for its exhibition of excellent horses.

"This wine," they explained, "is made without any fermentation, but simply by pressing the grapes, and by mixing 3 gallons of the pure juice with 1 gallon of apple brandy." And they estimated that an acre of ground well planted would yield twenty barrels. Reckoning labor costs of one hand per year per acre plus four hands for two weeks during the harvest season, the profits would probably run to $400 per acre. Their aspirations obviously bubbling, they intimated that they should be glad if one of Skinner's readers would send them a formula for "Champaigne." They ended by requesting that their names be withheld from "any public notice," but consented to sharing them privately with any of the editor's friends who might be "desirous of making any application for scions or wine."[44] Skinner came through nobly, got them a recipe for champagne, and headed their letter as follows:

SCUPPERNONG WINE

Manufacture and Sale of, in North Carolina
(The wine accompanying the following article
is truly a high flavoured, delicious beverage.)

But, after all, he was accustomed to doing favors, for it was he who arranged for the earliest publication of "The Star-spangled Banner," who encouraged naval officers to send home plants and seeds of possible value, helped to introduce Merino sheep, started the first magazine devoted to horse pedigrees and field sports in the United States, and even rounded up and shipped a few possums and wild turkeys to the family of Lafayette, for whose American interests he acted as a friendly agent.[45]

As the number of agricultural journals increased all over the nation there was, of course, a crescent opportunity to advertise one's products by describing one's success in missives gratefully received by editors often so harassed by the lack of original copy that they levied upon the other fellow's sheet in a manner that now seems shameless.[46] No one in North Carolina took advantage of the situation better than Sidney Weller, preacher and school teacher, who came from Orange County, New York, to Brinkleyville in Halifax County in the 1820s, bought a run-down farm of four hundred acres for $450, and in astonishing fashion built it into a model producer of field crops, with a thriving nursery and winery to boot.[47] He turned to winemaking, he insisted, with the customary apology, in order to advance the course of temperance. In 1840, when the sixth federal census showed North Carolina as leader of the Union in winemaking, his vineyard ranged over six acres, the largest in the state, so it was said, and nationally surpassed in volume only by the output of Nicholas Longworth near Cincinnati, who, with the aid of German immigrants and the Catawba grape, in time made the Ohio River an American Rhine. How relatively small the wine business then was, is indicated by the fact that shortly before his death in 1854 Weller's vineyard yielded forty to seventy barrels per year.

In 1848 his scuppernong sold at one to four dollars per gallon, the cheapest containing one-fourth spirits and the best three pounds of sugar per gallon. He appears to have included under the category scuppernong the "colored (or purple) Scuppernong, or muscadine, or bullus grapes," and declared the name to have been derived from an island in the Roanoke River. The muscadine grape was early called "Bullace," especially in South Carolina, because of its resemblance in appearance to a European

plum bearing that name. "Bull" grape is a corruption of the same, likewise "Bullet."[48]

Weller was selling the vines too, dispatching them as far away as
Natchez and St. Louis.* In 1853, in a report for the government, *The
Southern System of Vine Culture and Wine Making*,[49] he claimed to have
exhibited at local fairs scuppernongs measuring four inches in circumference and disclosed his formulas for making champagne, as well as hock
and Madeira out of them. Naturally, other vignerons had their own recipes, and there were those who adhered to Jefferson's view that the juice
did not require fortification. Such was J. Noyes, in Mississippi, who had
obtained vines from Weller and reported on his success with them. Obviously he was a bit crotchety, for he went out of his way to inform the
readers of the very influential *DeBow's Review*[50] (New Orleans-based) that
"the foolish name of Scuppernong, which it now holds in the Carolinas"
was an upstart, the correct name being Roanoke.

Weller developed a grape of his own, named it "Weller's Halifax," and
dispensed the plants with no little success, largely as a result of his contributing to "nearly every agricultural journal in the land." During the
silk craze that flared up again in the late 1830s and 40s he also profited
by the sale of mulberry trees. But the scuppernong grape provided the
essential basis of his fortunes. His enthusiastic accounts of profits to be
derived from it[51] stirred the imagination and encouraged others to set out
plants. "Grape of Grapes," "The Grape of the South"—such were the
phrases bandied about in encomiums of the scuppernong appearing in the
agricultural press, even in Florida, Alabama, and other once-remote regions of the Southland. They were often prompted by an amateur's luck
with the muscadine following hard upon a disastrous experience with the
vinifera.

More consequential than such amateurs to the story of our grape, however, may be three more physicians, all of whom, to use the frayed phrase,
helped to make history. The first of these to be considered here is Dr.
Samuel L. Mitchill, Columbia professor, legislator, long one of the editors of the *Medical Repository* (1729–1824), and now acclaimed among
"America's first great scientists."[52] He was made aware of the virtues of
the grape by one B. Blodgett, who wrote from Raleigh on January 6,
1829, telling the New York savant that he had recently returned from

*See Weller's account in *DeBow's*, V (Jan., 1848), 25–30, wherein he made clear that he could
ship grape vines "as a convenience for the South and South-west." "Wine-making as practiced in
North-Carolina," first read at a meeting of the American Agricultural Association, appeared in
Monthly Journal of Agriculture, I (1845), 243–46.

Alabama on a junket that had netted him fifty-two kinds of "spontaneous" grapes, of which he singled out the scuppernong "of Washington County in North Carolina" as especially worthy of note. There he had savored a delicious wine, fourteen years old, made of it by Captain William Burlingham, whose four-acre vineyard, cultivated for eighteen years, boasted a vine that produced "a tun of fruit," yielding "eight barrels of wine." After explaining the name, Blodgett promised to send on a cask of this phenomenal vintage. Mitchill doubtless liked it, too, for he had the letter published in the newly founded *New York Farmer and Horticultural Repository*, sponsored by the local horticultural society, whence it was reprinted far and wide.[53]

The second of our physicians is far more obscure than Dr. Mitchill but of more consequence to the annals of viticulture in America. Joseph Togno was his name. There is little record of him beyond his own communications to newspapers and horticultural periodicals. From them it appears that he had lived, perhaps was born, on the island of Corsica and possessed a rare collection of European treatises on the vine. His expertise was sufficient to enable him to take issue on details of viticulture with A. J. Downing, the famed landscape gardener, and with Nicholas Longworth, the most successful American vintner of his day. He had talked with Jefferson about his failures at Monticello with the *vinifera*, likewise with Bernard Laspeyre of Bladen County, Professor (later President) Joseph Caldwell in Chapel Hill, and Nicholas Herbemont of South Carolina, all of whom warned him that nobody could grow European grapes successfully in the United States. Togno, notwithstanding, resolved to set out a vineyard on a plantation near Wilmington called Diccoteaux.* His plants, "a choice collection," came from the estate of Le Comte Odart, "proprietor of the largest collection of grape-vines in the world," from whose "six thousand varieties" they were selected. (The count had rounded up exotic grapes for the French government and was the compiler of important works on the subject, including a standard ampelography.) On what particular basis Odart made the selections for Togno is not clear. But it is reasonable to infer that the doctor sent in exchange specimens of the various grapes native to the Cape Fear region. In all likelihood he sent the scuppernong abroad also.

To justify his stubbornness, he claimed that "so far back as 1821 and 1822," he had actually succeeded in cultivating the *vinifera* in Fauquier

---

*James Sprunt reports Togno's farm as having been leased from "Love Grove Plantation on Smith's Creek" (*Chronicles of the Cape Fear River*, 2d ed. [Raleigh, N.C., 1916], pp. 169–70).

County, Virginia, "on the farm of Dr. R. Peyton."[54] Most surprising of his endeavors, however, was the Vine Dressers' Model School, of which he was both founder and "Principal," a title he took no pains to conceal when communicating with editors.

Togno's efforts to educate Tarheels in the culture of the vine and to make Wilmington "the Bordeaux of America" deserve more than a passing word. Although he had had offers to settle in both Virginia and Kentucky, he reported, North Carolina was his choice because it was a land that "flows with the milk of human kindness and Scuppernong wine." He attended commencement exercises at Chapel Hill in June, 1849, to lecture on the need to introduce viticulture on "scientific principles" in the state, and the next year enlisted a galaxy of Wilmington's first citizens in the effort to get Secretary of State Daniel Webster to encourage American consuls in key places abroad to forward plants and cuttings for testing in his newly established vineyard.[55]*

Not only did he lecture in private and public on the economic advantages to be derived from the production of wines and raisins and the social benefits of horticultural improvements but zealously prepared the way for his school with a series of promotional letters, flowery in style and replete with quotations from Shakespeare, addressed to General Alexander MacRae, a prominent Wilmingtonian and railroad entrepreneur. These were printed at irregular intervals in the Wilmington *Commercial* during the summer and early autumn of 1849 (July 14, 17; August 2, 11; September 1, for example). In August his paid advertisement of the North Carolina Vine Dresser and Horticultural Model Practical School appealed to prospective patrons as follows:

"Construe the times to their necessities,
'Tis pride that pulls the country down"

The undersigned principal of said School is now ready to receive applications for pupils, over 14 years old, attended with or without a slave, to learn all the manipulations of the Vineyard, the orchard, and horticulture in general.

The pupils will be taught besides all the practical and scientific details of grape and fruitraising &c, the art of making wine, and of taking care of it at all periods of ripening, that of drying and preserving, out of season, the fresh fruit for the table use; the knowledge of soils and localities most advantageous to each plant; chemistry applied to agriculture in general, and especially to the prepa-

---

*Daniel Webster was to be approached through fellow cabinet member W. A. Graham of Hillsborough. A previous secretary had solicited such help for Togno, who paid shipping costs only to find most of the vines spoiled in transit (*The Papers of William A. Graham*, ed. J. G. deR. Hamilton [Raleigh, N.C., 1960], V, 393–96, 399–400).

ration and composition of the proper manure best suited to each kind of soil and production.

They will learn also, during leisure periods, the common branches of an English education as well as the French and Italian languages, in which the best treatises, on these subjects, are to be found. A geological and mineralogical cabinet will be formed by the pupils, by bringing specimens from their respective districts, which will become a subject of study and of practical knowledge and interest to the pupils. They shall keep a meteorological journal to habituate them to observe the effects of the vicissitudes of the Atmosphere on vegetation.

The principal has an extensive library for the use of the pupils.

When twenty pupils will be permanently secured for the space of three years, which is the time needed to acquire this business, I shall make the necessary preparations for their reception on the 1st. of January 1850. It is desired that early application should be made to enable the principal to make ample preparations for the accomodation of the pupils.

TERMS per year payable quarterly in advance.
  1. To the pupil's board and washing $170
  2. To tuition of the pupil bringing a slave, for all the above branches, and for the privilege of taking home, on the expiration of the 3d. Scholastic year, a stock of rooted vines and trees raised by the pupil himself $100
  3d. The pupil who has no slave at the School shall pay for the above Tuition &c $150
  4th. The board of the slave.[56]

His school apparently never prospered, but with his vineyard at first Togno appears to have had a bit of luck similar to his earlier attempt in Virginia. Eventually, however, his grafted vines succumbed to the bugs and blights and fungi, and he turned to the native grapes with avidity. His careful study of them is to be seen in a letter printed in the *Wilmington Herald* for November 10, 1851, in which he expertly discussed the origin of the Catawba, which he decided was the same as the Lincoln grape, secured from Senator Hanks of Lincoln County, N.C. The Isabella, likewise then attributed to a North Carolina origin, he flatly declared to be a cross with a European variety, an import from South Carolina. The *Herald* groaned editorially over the transfer of honors from the Old North State but doubtless recovered when the Report of the Commissioner of Patents promptly reprinted Togno's epistle.[57]*

As for the "Skoupernong," as Togno sometimes spelled the word, it meant in the Indian language "sweet water" (incidentally, a common be-

---

*Togno stated that he had learned from Dr. James F. McRee, whose memory extended as far back as 1810, that the Isabella was sold in Wilmington by Laspeyre, after whom the people in the area named it, though Laspeyre himself spoke of it as a foreign grape. Dr. McRee was a friend of Lyell and a correspondent of the Royal Society (Alfred M. Waddell, *A History of New Hanover County*, I. 43).

lief at the time), and of it there was "a purple variety called with us Bullus." When his French grapes petered out the doctor turned to the scuppernong with relief and proceeded to disseminate his admiration for it, at the same time explaining his methods and neatly advertising the Vine-Dressers' Model School at Diccoteaux.[58]

In the late 1850s, with a "grape-craze" in full swing and winemaking waxing in popularity and more widely distributed as new states came into production, the Bureau of Agriculture in Washington, then part of the Patent Office, undertook a careful study of grapes and enology in the various sections. Major John Le Conte, no mean authority, reporting in 1857 on the native grapes of the Atlantic states, concluded: "The Skuppernong, as I have known it in Georgia, is sweetest," but in North Carolina, where the wine is made "in large quantities," it is spoiled "by the infusion of whiskey, cider, spirits, or peach brandy, and after fermentation honey is often added"—the result being "a mixture of wine and half-fermented mead."[59] Two years later, samples of the most promising grapes then available were sent to Dr. Charles T. Jackson in Boston for chemical analysis, along with quite a few from New England, for several wine dealers in that area had backed the study with funds. Jackson, it may be remembered, was the physician-geologist-chemist who claimed the honor of introducing surgical anesthesia to the world; at the time he conducted a distinguished chemical laboratory where students were trained. Apparently, he liked the scuppernong best—despite a whiff of whiskey from the bottle containing the sample—so well, in fact, that he was led to expand his analysis as follows: "It has always been necessary to add a portion of brandy or some other spirit to keep the wine from souring; nevertheless, the Scuppernong wine is the best thus far produced in the United States. . . . With proper attention and care, Scuppernong wine may be made so fine as to excel all other wines made on this continent; and I would earnestly advise those interested to attend to the cultivation of this grape, in regions where the vine will grow, and make use of more skill in the manufacture. . . ."[60] *In regions where the vine will grow*—there was the rub. The muscadine could flourish only in the southern states. Moreover, what good was all this praise emanating from the very hotbed of abolition propaganda when these states were on the point of severing themselves from the Union? Long before Dr. Jackson turned from his flasks and beakers to write his report, a far more influential authority than he had ominously noted, in the first book on grape culture published in the nation: "Scuppernong—This does not bear fruit with me, it blossoms and the fruit forms in embryo, about the size of a pin's head, but never swells after; either the climate or soil does not suit it."[61] The critic was John Adlum of Georgetown, D.C., who, frustrated in his efforts to induce the federal authorities to establish an experimental vineyard, contented himself with his own farm. To it congressmen and visitors to the Capital rode out on sunny days, for it was one of the local sights. Presidents of the United States gravely commented on the wines he sent them to sample, and senators brought him seeds or cuttings from their bailiwicks to try out. Instead of the scuppernong, the wine grape that Adlum launched into national renown was the Catawba, by the introduction of which, he liked to say, he had contributed more to his country than if he had paid off the national debt.[62]*

It is perhaps symbolic that the national poet, Longfellow, wrote in praise of the Catawba while a mere regional poetaster, Paul H. Hayne, celebrated the muscadine. Even more poignant than the comparison is Longfellow's disclaimer, saying of his poem:

> It is not a song
> Of the Scuppernong
> From warm Carolinian valleys. . . .†

But one may, perhaps, be consoled by the fact that way up in Cambridge, Massachusetts, the Big White Grape was not unknown.

The Catawba, destined to be immensely popular in Ohio and New York, was not, however, the only rival of the Big White Grape to spring from the soil of North Carolina. There were also sister muscadines competing for honors among vintners and jelly makers before a century had rolled past the time that the Raleigh *Star* had announced its existence.[63] One was named for William Flowers, who came upon it first in 1816, in a swamp south of Lumberton. It was a great favorite during the 1870s, especially in Columbus County, where it was sometimes called the Babson.[64] There was also the Mish (or Meish), found by a farmer of that name near Washington, N.C., presumably in the 1840s. The lists of prizes offered by fairs in the old days often singled out the Mish and the Flow-

---

*A noted Carolina horticulturist, Silas McDowell, told the story of the finding of the Catawba, a few miles southeast of Asheville, in a letter to the alleged discoverer, Colonel William Murray (*Southern Cultivator*, XVII [1859], 246–47).

†"Catawba Wine" was inspired by the vintage made by Nicholas Longworth near Cincinnati. The Victorian journalist Charles MacKay also penned a poetic "Catawba," calling the wine "the nectar and balm of the West" (*Illustrated London News*, XXXII [March 20, 1858] 297). The literary world was alerted to the scuppernong and Catawba during the grape craze of the 1850s by a long article, "American Wines," which appeared in the November and December, 1854, issues of *Putnam's Monthly* (IV, 504–11, 611–19).

ers, along with the scuppernong, for special awards; and, later, these favorites were joined by the James, a large purplish grape of delicious flavor and splendid keeping quality named for the one who discovered it in Pitt County—in 1866, some say.[65] This last has become such a favorite that many North Carolinians have assumed that all dark-skinned muscadines are James grapes. And dwellers in the eastern counties or the Piedmont who do not rely on the spontaneous offerings of the woods and fields are still planting both a James and a scuppernong so as to have the best of the two colors.

These are but a few of the better-known varieties from within the state. To these may be added, for example, the Pee Dee and the Thomas from South Carolina. Moreover, the ingenious plant breeders of recent years have contributed many more varieties of muscadines of size, color, and taste to suit almost anybody's palate. But the scuppernong is still North Carolina's grape. And with it the story of commercial winemaking in the United States began a new phase.

Dr. Calvin Jones (*courtesy Division of Archives and History, Raleigh, N.C.*)

Wharton J. Green, owner of Tokay Vineyard near Fayetteville
(*courtesy Manuscript Division, Perkins Library, Duke University*)

CHAPTER II

Wines and Vines in the Old North State

When the Civil War ended, the prospect of the scuppernong's becoming more than a sectional favorite among the relatively few Americans who looked upon the wine when it was red—or white—seemed paltry indeed. The *rotundifolia* could be grown successfully only in portions of the southern states, and there the labor force was suddenly disrupted, the transportation system wrecked, and the ruling class demoralized if not bankrupted. Yet there were those who proclaimed that a farmer bereft of his slaves could still forge ahead as vineyardist or orchardist. The scuppernong was the grape to plant because of the minimal labor requisite to a sucessful crop. Furthermore, southern nurserymen were to be patronized, on the grounds not only of regional loyalty but because nursery stock from Yankeeland carried "the yellows" and other diseases. As late as 1888 J. W. Vandiver of Weaverville, N.C., continued to introduce his annual catalog with a Confederate homily.[1] Sectional prejudice had manifested itself in horticulture long before the war, as S. W. Westbrook, the only southerner to attend the first meeting of the National Pomological Society in Rochester, N.Y., made clear to the North Carolina Agricultural Society at its 1858 assembly.[2] Even George Husmann, "the pioneer scientific winegrower in Missouri," in 1870 attacked the scuppernong, declaring he had tasted it just once, an experience that reminded him "of the bugs we sometimes get in our mouth accidentally when picking raspberries or strawberries"—a calumny for which a grower from Alabama quickly took him to task.[3] The word *foxy*—sometimes *catty*—was frequently used in the North in derogation of the muscadine, a dishonor often shared by all the other eastern grapes in the vocabulary particularly of Californians.

Despite the prejudices of those who believed, or professed to believe, that good wine can be made only from the European *vinifera*, it is probably the foxiest of our native grapes that has come closest to the rating of national grape, namely, the Concord.* Its taste is what most Americans think of when they speak of grape flavor. Its celebrity is largely due to the immense terrain, North or South, on which it flourishes and its appeal to manufacturers of jellies and nonalcoholic drinks. The popularity of its juice owes more than a little to a dentist named Thomas B. Welch, who by 1870 had gone into business with his son in producing "Dr. Welch's Unfermented Wine," as it was first called. The dentist was a wine-hating steward in a Methodist church in Vineland, New Jersey.[4] But among American wine drinkers it was the muscadine—and neither the Concord nor any California *vinifera*—whose flavor dominated the most popular vintage consumed in the United States during the two decades before national Prohibition.[5]

In tracing the progress of the scuppernong toward national prominence one may easily stray from the outline path of historical narrative and bog down in parochial details, especially when, as here in the present chapter, the intention is to confine the story to one state. Few rural Carolinians need to be reminded that where one vine grew on a trellis back of a farmhouse a dozen flourished spontaneously in the neighboring woods, or that in most households the only bottle of wine likely to be found on the shelf was intended as medicine—more rarely as flavoring for the Christmas fruitcake or perhaps a bowl of syllabub. With the hot weather prevalent during the vintage season and the lack of proper storage facilities, why risk making wine anyhow? Unless one were a foreigner like the pioneer Moravians† or the Waldensians a century later, there was small likelihood that anyone in the family knew the art. The crowds of German and Italian immigrants who as consumers or vintners encouraged winemaking in Ohio, New York, and California generally gave the South a wide berth. If any alcoholic beverage was made in the neighborhood the chances were that it was applejack or whiskey or, more humbly, bland persimmon beer, sometimes called "Possum Toddy." Long after the Civil War the typical vintner in the region was a Negro woman who had learned a formula from "Old Missy," who in turn had found it in a "Creole cookbook" or perhaps "Grandma's old batch of recipes." The few families that subscribed to the early agricultural journals, often derided as "book

---

*In 1868 the Concord was selected as best winegrape for Ohio and best table grape for the nation (*American Agriculturist*, XXVII [November, 1868], 414).

†In 1769 three settlements of Carolina Moravians made nineteen hogsheads from "the great abundance of wild grapes" (*Guide Book of North-Western North Carolina* [Salem, N.C., 1878], p. 103). That same year the Fathers brought the first Mission grapes into California. Valdese, N.C. was the seat of a flourishing winery for many years.

farmers," could, however, find directions for winemaking with little difficulty in their pages.

As for commercial wineries in North Carolina, several dating from the old regime, like that founded by Sidney Weller at Brinkleyville, were revived after the Civil War and usually operated on a larger scale. Manufacturing of all sorts was, of course, handicapped by the paucity of cities and the inadequacy of transportation as well. And even when the spread of railroads was quickened as the New South rose from the ashes of the Old and faster packetboats fostered waterborne traffic, commerce in alcoholic beverages was overhung by the ascending nimbus of the "prohibition sentiment." Improvements in transportation, however, stimulated a corresponding growth in truck- and fruit-raising, first in the region closest to Norfolk and later where railways served areas possessed of the proper soil.

An enclave of fruit growers, many of foreign birth, briefly existed in the 1870s near Ridgeway, where the *American Farmer* for August, 1873, reported "a large fruit-drying factory" with several peach orchards and "over a hundred acres in vines" in the vicinity. But, as the same journal reported in June, 1876, the grapes came to nought, the chief experimenters, the firm of J. L. Labiaux and Clerc, losing all of their varieties, "a hundred thousand vines" of *vinifera* all told. The peaches did better.

After recovering from the depression of 1873 the fresh fruit business prospered. A mighty impetus was added late in the century when refrigerated units of a modern type supplanted the iced crates stored in ordinary box or express cars. The Chicago-based California Fruit Transportation Company, then primarily concerned with shipments from the lower Mississippi region to the Midwest, eventually extended operations also into the Carolinas. In 1892 from the Wilmington-Goldsboro area it moved forty-three carloads; four years later the number jumped to 290.* Strawberries and vegetables such as green peas, to be sure, accounted for most of this traffic. On a smaller scale vineyardists and fruitgrowers also profited by these expedited shipments of fresh produce to New York and other northern cities. The North Carolina Fruitgrowers' Association was established in 1879 primarily to obtain better freight rates from the railway companies.[6] At its annual fair held in August, 1886, in Fayetteville, more than a hundred kinds of apples and 116 varieties of grapes were

---

*From an advertisement appearing in James Sprunt, *Tales and Traditions of the Lower Cape Fear, 1661–1896* ([Wilmington, N.C., 1896], p. lv). Railways often issued publications promoting truck- and fruit-raising. The Seaboard Air Lines booklet on *The Sand Hills Area of the Carolinas* (Norfolk, Va., n.d.) dwells on grapes particularly.

displayed, S. W. Noble of New Hanover accounting for seventy-five of the latter and a Mr. Batchelor of Wake County, fifty-eight.[7] The fresh-fruit market was then booming.

Grapes for the basket trade were largely of the bunch varieties, and many of the vines were originally bought from northern nurserymen, principally Concords and Niagaras. Certain vineyards were planted also with wine-making varieties including muscadines. These helped to assure a supply of grapes for the presses, along with any market grapes too inferior to command respectable prices. In case of a glutted market the whole crop could sometimes thus be salvaged. The wine was usually re-tailed in the neighborhood or wholesaled to larger winemakers. The fed-eral census of manufactures for 1900 listed 187 of these latter for Califor-nia, fifty-two for Ohio, thirty-eight for New York, and, in the South, six for Georgia and five for North Carolina. It was the custom for the smaller vineyardists, and a necessity for the larger operators, in the South upon occasion to purchase blackberries as well as muscadines from such folk, principally blacks, as were willing to scour the fields and woods to gather them. As of June 1, 1900, the Census reported 1,213,897 vines in the state and the previous harvest as 12,344,001 pounds of grapes. Wines made on the reporting farms were estimated at 146,699 gallons. As is the case today, a few Carolinians made wine as a hobby. Many more took to their stills—but not as a hobby.

Despite shipping qualities inferior to those of the James, hand-picked scuppernongs occasionally reached consumers in New York and Balti-more. Ordinarily they were packaged in berry boxes or slat baskets, though at least one farmer in Chowan County tried paper containers. Another ardent soul, J. W. Page, boasted that as early as 1850 he had shipped them to Maine by packing them on alternate layers of cotton. Page also recalled that agents of Nicholas Longworth "in the years just before the war" bought up scuppernong juice in the Pamlico and Albe-marle regions "to impart flavor and a *bouquet* not otherwise obtainable, to his celebrated Cincinnati wines."[8] That agents from Ohio were involved is not corroborated, but the shipments by rail of juice, like the transport of fresh fruits, increased steadily.

Apart from commission merchants, the men engaged in the wine busi-ness in nineteenth-century North Carolina seem to have come and gone with the snows of yesteryear. In Columbus County, where bunch grapes fared poorly but muscadines flourished, a pioneer vintner was Colonel Alfred Smith. About 1870 at Whiteville, originally named Vineland, the firm of Ellis and Company became noted as a chief supplier. Primarily a nursery, it was bought out in 1872 by one of its participant partners, Colonel T. S. Memory, who continued to operate it until his death in 1896. A seedling, of a Thomas grape presumably, found in his vineyard was given his name, and the Memory grape was widely planted as far off as Texas. In Florida about 1910 it was considered the "best all-around black variety" of muscadine.[9] In 1904 the Whiteville Wine Company exhibited scuppernong wine at the Louisiana Purchase Exposition held in St. Louis.

In the countryside served by Wilmington, where Dr. Togno, all too briefly, had acted as missionary for good wines and scientific viticulture, S. W. Noble, mentioned above, was among the oustanding growers. A Castle Hayne Vineyard Company existed in the 1870s. Far surpassing all rival winemakers in the vicinity was the family of Sol Bear, who, in 1853, had established a wholesale business in household furnishings, dry goods, etc. which soon handled alcoholic beverages as well.[*] By 1902 the Bears employed six commercial travelers and had an agent in New York, for their business ranged far beyond the state. In addition to imported liquors of all sorts, they dispensed local apple brandy, corn whiskey, and the native wines. A brand of rye rectified by them was named Breezeland, and one of their featured vinous products was the Belle of Carolina, which resembled a mild port. Blackberries and muscadines of all sorts provided the ingredients for their several wines, sold for the most part to licensed dealers in case lots at prices ranging upwards from six dollars each. Their liquor business increased apace and resulted in a new winery, built about 1912 at Front and Marsteller Streets and capable of turning out 200,000 gallons a year.[10] The Bears' plant was one of the largest consumers of muscadines in the nation, and its demands, fortified by those of Paul Garrett and others, already by 1906 practically exhausted the available supply of scuppernongs, the grapes much preferred of all the *rotundifolia* for winemaking. Growers tried to palm off the juice of other varieties under its honored name, and "pure scuppernong" was likely to be "pure muscadine."

In 1887 the North Carolina Department of Agriculture undertook a chemical analysis of wines, conducted by F. P. Venable and W. B. Phillips of the University.[11] Carolina manufacturers represented were C. W.

---

[*] Revered patriarch of the Wilmington synagogue, Sol Bear presided over the third annual meeting of the Liquor Dealers, Distillers, and Grape Growers Association of the state held in Asheville in 1895.

Garrett and Company of the Medoc Vineyards (Sidney Weller's successors); N. W. Craft, a professional nurseryman with more than a million trees, shrubs, and vines at Shore in Yadkin County; H. Mahler of Raleigh; and G. W. Lawrence of the Happy Valley Vineyard, near Fayetteville, both primarily vineyardists.* In 1893 the Carolina wines exhibited at the Columbian Exposition in Chicago came from the Medoc Vineyards, the Engadine Vineyard in Buncombe County, George Schellum in Raleigh, G. W. Lawrence, mentioned earlier, and Wharton J. Green at Fayetteville. Several of these from time to time sent samples of their wines to expositions as far away as Paris and Vienna—and occasionally received awards.

The Fayetteville neighborhood was long renowned for its wines, some of its vineyards predating the Civil War. In the 1870s T. S. Lutterloh was noted for his well-kept vines on a plot seven miles west of the city.[12]† George W. Lawrence's vineyard, Happy Valley, was located on the Raleigh Road; it had been bought by him in 1863 from Robert Wooten. Another of longer standing, called the Bordeaux, came into the possession of James H. Pearce, who marketed the bountiful harvest from some five hundred mature scuppernongs principally in the western counties.[13] Far more distinguished was the Tokay Vineyard, pride and joy of Colonel Wharton J. Green, soldier, congressman, lawyer, and courtly host whose many guests remembered with delight the bouquet from the scuppernong served at his table and the brandy tinctured with the flavor of fruit that accompanied his choice Havanas. His, too, was an old vineyard, dating from the 1840s, with the Big White Grape in 1860 dominating some thirty acres planted by a genial chap, M. T. Horne, whose nickname "Jolly" did not prevent him from being strung up by Sherman's soldiers, presumably because he objected too strenuously to handing over the keys to his cellar. Cut down by a servant, he survived only a few months, and, in 1865, his property came into the hands of his nephew Henry R. Horne, a druggist and later an officer of the state pharmaceutical society. An experienced vintner, Allen McBuie, restored and improved the business and was retained as superintendent when the affable

*North Carolina had been one of the first states to hire a chemist for agricultural investigation. Analysis, at the outset centered on fertilizers, was located in Chapel Hill (Ira P. Schaub, *North Carolina Agricultural Experiment Station: The First Sixty Years, 1877–1937* [Raleigh, N.C., 1955], pp. 117 ff.).

†The family had been in the nursery business since the 1850s. By 1857 C. Lutterloh had issued the 4th edition of his *Catalog of Select . . . Plants*.

and wealthy Colonel purchased it in 1879 and gave it the official name Tokay Wine Company.

By 1885 it was a showplace, situated on a broad tableland some three miles from Fayetteville. Thirty-odd varieties of grapes made neat patterns on a hundred acres, and rumor had it that the Colonel's place was "the largest vineyard this side of the Rockies." Scuppernongs and the allied Mish and Flowers grapes predominated, while Nortons and Cynthianas came next. Production ranged annually from twenty to thirty-five thousand gallons, of twelve different varieties, with a total storage capacity of a hundred thousand, of which almost half was ready for shipping. The main warehouse was sixty by seventy-five feet; the cellar had a hard clay floor; four fermenting tanks held three thousand gallons each; storage casks ranged from six to nine hundred gallons in capacity; and shipping casks averaged 110 to 250 gallons. Both warehouse and cellar were heated by steam, and a small still of the most modern design stood ready for action.

The Tokay's wines, it was firmly announced, came solely from American grapes and were made without adulteration or artificial flavoring. This latter point was a matter of special note, for as a member of Congress active in promoting the incipient pure-wine legislation of the times[14] Green had had a hand in exposing "the ramified and pernicious extent" to which adulteration of imported wines had been carried on. In a florid "Essay on American Grape Culture," he bewailed the not uncommon practice of exporting California wines to France and shipping them back with French labels, argued for tax benefits for American producers on the ground that they avoided "the tricks of the trade of the Old-World culturist," and extolled the juice of the scuppernong as one of the most delicious in the world, possessed, moreover, of "aperient and diuretic qualities" recommended by the medical profession. He also lamented the practice of degrading the wine of the noble scuppernong into a syrup "by the profuse artificial addition of sugar."[15]

A sample of the Colonel's oratory shows reason for his popularity in North Carolina. It comes from his remarks made in the House on April 21, 1884:

Mr. Speaker, under the operation of our delectable revenue laws, as at present enforced, there are grievous penalties attaching to illicit distillation, as many of the poor mountaineers in my own poor State know full well to their cost. Now, sir, I opine that if the restrictions on distillation, including tax on the legitimate article and pains and penalties on the illicit or "moonshine," were removed altogether, and these makers of a pure article of whiskey and brandy left as free as their fathers were in that regard, and the same punishments doubled or quadrupled meted out to the compounders of the poisonous stuffs engendered by the tricks of chemistry, the cause of morality and the sanitary cause, not to say the cause of liberty and sobriety, would be materially subserved thereby.[16]

The Tokay Vineyard's wines were labeled as Dry Red, Dry White, Sweet Red, and Sweet White and were thought to resemble Spanish and Madeira vintages. The Sweet White, a contemporary connoisseur declared, had a more delicate bouquet than the similar California Mission wine, then regarded with more esteem than now. Green's vineyard put out also the conventional Concord, Norton, port, claret, sherry, and the like.

The estate included an eight-acre peach orchard, whose fruit was packed for shipping to the North, and four breeding ponds, near a large natural lake, well stocked, where the Colonel passed leisure hours with hook and line. While in many ways Wharton J. Green kept up the manner of living of the old-school southerner, he was a gentleman of the new school, too, if one may judge by the fact that water was pumped into his house by steam power and gas "of home production" lighted the premises. His wines must have ranked among the best ever made in North Carolina.

Residents in or near Raleigh had planted scuppernongs ever since the first seeds were forwarded by Blount from Washington County or they had sampled the Pettigrew vintages brought from the shore of Phelps Lake. Their wine was in all likelihood made for home consumption until professional orchardists and vignerons came upon the scene, new varieties of trees and vines were set out, and the demand for fresh fruit brought on a rash of small suppliers. By the eighties there existed a county grape-growers' association. There was also a Wake County Farmers' Institute, at whose meeting in the city in 1887 a prominent pomologist, S. Otho Wilson, demonstrated methods of planting and pruning vines,* and Dr. W. C. Dabney explained how to make a novel something called bordeaux mixture and showed off his "spraying apparatus." This phenomenon was the "second machine of its kind" in the whole nation, so it was said, the other being in Washington, the property of the U.S. Department of Agriculture.[17] In Raleigh the Concord was favored for the basket market.

---

*Wilson also ran the Raleigh Nurseries, which listed among its grapes the Concord, Flowers, Hartford Prolific, Ives, and the scuppernong, "undoubtedly the best grape in cultivation" (*Descriptive Catalog for 1879–80* [Raleigh, N.C., 1879]).

The nurserymen and professionals, like J. Van Lindley, who reported their recommendations to their fellows of the newly established State Horticultural Society called it "the lazy man's grape," productive of "fruit without work."[18] Before long it became apparent that bordeaux mixture was a boon—and even useful for occasional application on the tried and true scuppernongs, of which most experienced growers retained at least a few.

The high season for the fresh grape shipments began ordinarily in mid-July and lasted about a month, marking a period between the end of the Florida crop and the beginning of that of Virginia. In 1893 it was estimated that 359 acres in the Raleigh neighborhood were in production of about 90,000 baskets, usually holding ten pounds each, Ives grapes running a distant second to the Concords, with many fewer Delawares, Niagaras, and others. H. Mahler and George Schellum, both probably Germans, with twenty acres each, were more widely recognized as vintners than most of their neighboring growers—among whom were farmers, nurserymen, and people like Commissioner of Agriculture John Robinson or Judge Walter Clark.[19]

Bunch grapes were of course the mainstay of the western counties where the climate suited the *labruscas*, and apples were far and away of more consequence in commerce. But as early as the 1850s Silas McDowell conducted at Franklin notable experiments with hybrids that gave promise of surpassing the Catawba in the region of its birth. He tried also to improve the Isabella, cuttings of which he had obtained from Cherokee Indians.* Another early fancier in the western section was William Murdock, who offered fifty dollars to anyone who would procure for him a new native grape superior to the Catawba.[20] Later, Captain J. K. Hoyt, at the Engadine Vineyard, fifteen miles west of Asheville, as we have seen, produced a superior wine often exhibited at fairs, including the international one held in St. Louis in 1904. And occasionally a foreigner such as a Swiss named Golay at Old Fields did likewise. As a result of the favorable thermal belt surrounding it, a widely heralded center for grapes was developed near Tryon in the nineties, and Polk County ranked third in the number of its vines when the census reported 1,213,897 for the whole state as of 1899. Halifax County ranked second, but far in the lead with 396,813 vines stood Moore County.

Enticed by the prospects of higher prices to be derived from earlier harvests in the favorable climate of the Sand Hills, farmers and nursery-

*Several apples from the Cherokee country were given Indian names, like Nickajack. For other such names, see *Southern Cultivator*, XVII (1859), 284.

men reclaimed hundreds of acres, often of blackjack scrub, left in the wake of lumbering operations and planted them with peaches, berries, and grapes. The portion of Moore County near Southern Pines was soon transformed. The Niagara Vineyard Company alone set out 250 acres, and the Southern Pines Vineyard likewise joined the van. Niagaras and Delawares were much in evidence along with the Concords—all these for the basket trade primarily. Scuppernongs, too, were in favor, for the large grape-processing plant at Aberdeen nearby paid very good prices for them.

Prices for muscadines, like those for others, varied considerably according to the whims of the seasons. Hand-picked fruit, attractively packed, commanded higher prices than similar grapes shattered from the vines onto canvas sheets, or picked up from the ground, and shipped in barrels to a pressing plant. Shortly after the turn of the century wineries averaged between eighty-five cents and a dollar per bushel for shattered grapes. Choice, hand-picked muscadines in half-bushel peach baskets or in berry boxes ranged from one to two dollars a bushel. James and Mish varieties were the best shippers but the scuppernong was the top favorite with the wineries. In 1906 when a North Carolina farmer harvested 177 bushels per acre from a four-year-old patch of James grapes no one believed that a miracle had taken place. Muscadines paid.

In 1913, to encourage business, the manager of the Southern Pines Grape Nurseries, R. C. Cool, issued a pamphlet containing advice to prospective growers of the scuppernongs. By way of introduction he reminded his readers that the "great deal" of interest in the grape engendered during "the last few years" was due solely to a flourishing market. And in a concluding summary he maintained, "We know of no other fruit that combines the safety of market with the low cost of production and large crops." No insects, no expenses for pruning, no danger from late frosts, "no age limit to the vines"—planting such a grape, he concluded, "takes the industry out of the gamble class."[21] What an inducement, especially to those who had heard of the three dollars per bushel actually paid by the wineries for the Big White Grapes only two years before!

In addition to the Pinehurst resort built on sandy acres bought in 1895 from the family of Walter Hines Page by James W. Tufts, the soda-fountain millionaire, there was also in the same corner of Moore County a remarkable experimental farm laid out in motley patches with vegetables, berries, peaches, and grapes. This was a joint project, initiated in 1895,

Mahler's Vineyard near Raleigh, N.C. (*courtesy N.C. Museum of Natural History*)

The Niagara Company's vineyard near Southern Pines
(courtesy N.C. Museum of Natural History)

and backed by the German Kali works, the state authorities, the Horticultural Society, and independent growers. The purpose was to determine just which chemicals best promoted the growth and fruiting of the various horticultural products of commercial consequence to the region. Both before the participants parted company and afterwards, bulletins, with before-and-after pictures, publicized the findings, and these, along with the eye-witness accounts of numerous visitors, aided the advance of horticulture in the Sand Hills.[22] While state agencies came far short of California authorities in promoting viticulture, North Carolina was not altogether negligent. When in 1890 W. F. Massey was appointed as the first horticulturist to serve in the North Carolina State Agricultural Experiment Station (founded in 1877) he noted that 115 kinds of grapes were already under observation.[23]

Most important for scuppernong growers was a long-sustained and carefully supervised investigation of all phases of muscadine culture, begun in 1905 by federal authorities in cooperation with state officials and centered primarily at Willard, N.C., in Pender County. Phases of the study involved growers in North Carolina, Florida, and elsewhere, as well as botanists and chemists in Washington. George C. Husmann, whose father had defamed the Big White Grape, was the pomologist in general charge, and W. A. Taylor headed the federal division of field investigation. As the latter explained to the editor of the *Progressive Farmer*,[24] one of the first efforts was to identify and assemble all promising varieties, many of which were unknown outside the immediate locale in which they were discovered, to compare their merits, test the best lands for commercial potentialities, and learn how to grow them most efficiently. The outbreak of World War I delayed the completion of the study. At the outset it was quickly learned that three-fifths of all muscadines were made into wine and that the white-skinned ones commanded the highest prices. The two largest plants then making such wine, at Wilmington (Sol Bear's family) and Norfolk (Paul Garrett), alone insured an unfailing demand for them.

The traditional view that no pruning was necessary was shown to be superstitious nonsense, as was also the belief that the bees and the bugs could be left to take care of fertilizing the blossoms. Nature's ten percent of success with the bloom buds could readily be raised to thirty-five or more by the use of pollinators. The size of berries or clusters could be wondrously enlarged and the summer drop-off considerably lessened by breeding. In time a rash of improved varieties emerged in the wake of this and subsequent studies, including one appropriately named Willard. By the time national Prohibition arrived, the federal Agricultural Department, the best friend the muscadines ever had, could show beyond a shadow of doubt that the test farm in Pender County outstripped all rival vineyards in the region. All varieties were heartily recommended for jellies, preserves, and catsup, and when canned, it was concluded, they were good for use in pies. Uncle Sam also passed the word along that the old backwoods custom of drying the skins for pie making later in the winter worked quite successfully. In 1920, to jump ahead for a moment, the department announced that the use of muscadine grape juice and marmalade was on the increase, thanks to the efforts of its home-demonstration agents and those of the state agricultural colleges. During the previous Christmas season the dining car superintendents of three principal railways obtained "large quantities" and had had to telegraph for more.* But it took a lot of marmalade to take up the slack caused by the closing of the wineries.

The horticultural map of the Old North State was dotted in a multitude of places other than those already used for illustration. The grape growers in Wilson County made a kind of cluster—but more often than not a single dot represented a vintner with a small press, like the ancient one on the old Cannon farm at Chapel Hill, or a professional such as S. R. Hunt in Granville County or the owner of the initials E. M. W. who had 56 acres of muscadines in Craven County in 1869. In the Charlotte area there was a more ambitious devotee, Daniel Asbury, who in 1871 gathered 129 pounds of ripe fruit from one four-year-old vine in his seven-acre plot of *labruscas*. No wonder that he planned to set out 24,000 new vines the next year.[25] Unless their habits had changed, it is doubtful that his fruit would have passed his neighbors' throats in the shape of wine, if one may judge by Dr. John B. Alexander's recollections of old days there. Corn whiskey, he recalled, was the "standing drink for both winter and summer. . . . Peach brandy was an aristocratic drink, especially if it was sweetened with honey. . . . Only a few people made wine, but some did indulge in blackberry, and a few in domestic grape wine, but to no great extent. . . ." Cherry bounce, likewise, was distinctly "aristocratic." It was made "by putting the common black cherry, with an admixture of a few wild cherries into a demijohn, and then pouring on a

*Scuppernong juice, it was learned, while most delectable when fresh, lost quality when heat was used to extract the fluid from the seeds or to pasteurize the free flow (*New York Times*, May 10, 1920, p. 13).

good article of rye whiskey or peach brandy, whatever the vessel would hold and adding enough sugar and cloves to suit the taste." [26]

In Lincoln County, long believed to have originated a grape of its own, the Lincoln Wine Company as early as 1871 made a practice of selling the output of its fourteen acres in New York. More ambitious was the Land Owner's Company in Warren County which maintained a thousand acres in peaches, planted in 1868 or 1869, and thirty in grapes. Another giant was the Excelsior Planting Company of Rocky Point in New Hanover County with seventy-one acres in vines, mostly Concord but some Mish and scuppernong. [27] Their peach, apple, and pear orchards were more extensive. Obviously, fruit growing was a factor in the springtime of the New South.

Halifax County continued to be the most important North Carolina center for the production of scuppernong wine. By 1900 it reported more than twice as many vines as Wilson County, and most of them were muscadines. In September, 1893, the editor of the Weldon *Roanoke News* complained that so many grape skins were littering the streets that an ordinance was needed to cope with the aggravating situation. One could drive out in any direction and find a farm where one could eat his fill for fifteen cents—twenty-five if he had his girl along. [28] Much of the abundance stemmed from plants a generation old bought from Sidney Weller. But a more recent contributor to the uberous profusion was a German happily named Louis Froelich, who by instruction and example passed on to others his own missionary zeal for what he called "the most profitable grape in the world." Twenty years' experience on the slopes of the Rhineland had prepared him to appreciate the relative freedom from disease and the immense fecundity of the muscadines. Moreover, he had tried out both *vinifera* grafts and *labruscas* on his original fourteen-acre plot at Kenansville in Duplin County before making his decision to set out 150 acres of his favorites near Enfield in Halifax. Furthermore, within a two-year period prior to 1871 he had put in some five thousand muscadines for others. From time to time he explained his methods for the benefit of the readers of the farm journals, and the authorities in Washington likewise publicized his comments on grapes and wines. [29]

This nurseryman-vintner grew ten sorts of muscadines, several of which were made into a sparkling vintage which he shipped, usually after a second racking, to New York. There it was bottled and sold as champagne. He conscientiously experimented with the procedures employed in planting, spacing, manuring, and pruning and adapted the time-honored techniques of the Rhineland to the requirements of Carolina cellars. Of his ten different varieties the top-ranking grape in saccharine strength was his own Froelich's White Seedling; next came its progenitor, the Common White Scuppernong, as he called it. Either produced a delicious straw-colored wine. In addition to the Mish, Flowers, Thomas, and ordinary Black Scuppernong, his others bore names like Pamlico, Beaufort, Tenderpulp, and Sugar. The two latter originated as seedlings near Whiteville, whence they had presumably come into his possession via the firm of Ellis and Company of that city.[30] The Beaufort made a purplish wine; the others, a red. The care with which he selected only the best berries and the pains he bestowed upon the extraction of their juice must have astonished his neighbors, as did, no doubt, his refusal to adulterate his product. Like all good vineyardists of the day, he had also a still.

The most distinguished winery in North Carolina history was another ornament to Halifax County, namely the Medoc Vineyards, started by Sidney Weller and long identified with the Garretts, a family of yeoman planters originally located in Edgecombe County. It was from its midst that one of the all-time giants in the annals of American enology arose, Paul Garrett. He it was who made the flavor of the Big White Grape known all over the nation under the name of Virginia Dare. These ventures warrant a separate chapter.

CHAPTER III

The Garretts

The Medoc, as it came to be called, was the most historic winery in North Carolina. It was purchased in 1867 by C. W. Garrett and Company, as successors to the enterprise which had made its founder, Sidney Weller, the leading vintner of the South of the 1840s. Charles W. Garrett, chief owner and manager, had prospered in a clothing business in New York City and returned to North Carolina following the outbreak of the Civil War. At the instance of Governor Zeb Vance he took charge of the procurement of uniforms for the state's soldiers and after Appomattox returned to the North to retrieve his property. It was not long before failing health forced his retirement and he bought the concern at Ringwood, apparently along with his brother, the physician Dr. Francis Marion Garrett. It was called the Ringwood Wine Company, and its letterhead advertised "Pure Scuppernong" and "Imperial Champagne" in particular, though it produced other kinds of wine also, as well as the usual brandy and vinegar. Traveling salesmen took orders, principally in towns and cities in the South, and most of the sales were in bulk.* Sound bookkeeping practices were introduced, distribution was revamped, more vines were planted, and various winemakers were employed in succession, among them apparently a German, a Swiss, and a Frenchman. The Negro help, most of it seasonal, satisfied with their wages, were encouraged to sing spirituals under the leadership of a quartet of cellar men permanently employed because of their vocal talents as well as their manual dexterity. As the business grew, more grapes were obtained in the forty-mile area surrounding.

The federal Department of Agriculture's report for 1871 described the vineyard as comprised of 8,000 scuppernongs, 2,000 Concords, and much smaller numbers of Delawares, Ionas, etc. From only 400 of the older scuppernongs, covering five acres, the annual yield ranged from

---

* A few letters of C. W. Garrett and Spooner Harrison dating from the 1870s are in the Southern Historical Collection of the University of North Carolina Library.

three to five thousand gallons, sold at a dollar per gallon for still wine and ten dollars per dozen bottles for sparkling. Twenty years later the total capacity of the Medoc was estimated at 175,000 gallons plus some brandy. In 1883 when the State Board of Agriculture authorized payments for a display of North Carolina's products at an exposition held in Boston, the firm sent "aged brandy," four crates of fresh Mish grapes, and wines described as follows: "Claret, extra dry Claret, old native Claret [probably from wild muscadines], Norton's Virginia Seedling Claret, Mish, Scuppernong, Red Imperial and old native Port."* The preponderance of clarets in this shipment may be explained by the fact that claret cups and claret lemonade were among the most popular beverages in the polite circles of the era.

Early in the present century the Medoc Vineyards produced not only White Imperial Scuppernong, Imperial Champagne, and other vintages from that grape but also wines made from the Mish, port from the latter being a favorite with customers in Boston. Blackberry and Catawba were also on their list, and their brandy, made from the scuppernongs, was recommended to druggists with the reminder that it had been awarded a diploma at the Atlanta Exposition (1895) attesting its merits for medicinal purposes.[1]

The doctor's son Paul about 1877 was inducted into the business and proceeded in fabulous style to learn both the bookkeeping and the production aspects of its operations. He had had fairly good schooling in the usual military academy and was coached in Latin by his father. As a husky lad of fourteen he sang along with the blacks and showed them how neatly a heavy cask could be maneuvered onto a drag to be hauled off to the railway station.† It was the intention of his elders that he would take over the management upon the death of his uncle. But, instead, a son-in-law of Charles Garrett was put in charge, and soon displayed such incompatibility that young Paul left Ringwood to assume a job as a salesman, acting under the direction of a pair of brothers named Wright who were the principal travelers for the Ringwood Wine Company though they were also selling cigars and other products for the Brown Tobacco Company, likewise a North Carolina firm. Their most lucrative territory

---

*Other exhibitors were Colonel Green of the Tokay Vineyard, S. R. Hunt and Co. of Kittrells in Granville County, and the Seaboard Wine Company, apparently owned by the railroad (C. W. Dabney, *Catalogue of the North Carolina Exhibit at Boston, 1883* [Raleigh, N.C., 1884], p. 57).

†Paul Garrett dictated reminiscences and yarns of his earliest activities just prior to his death in 1940. A Xerox copy is deposited in the Perkins Library at Duke University through the kindness of his daughter, Mrs. L. J. Barden.

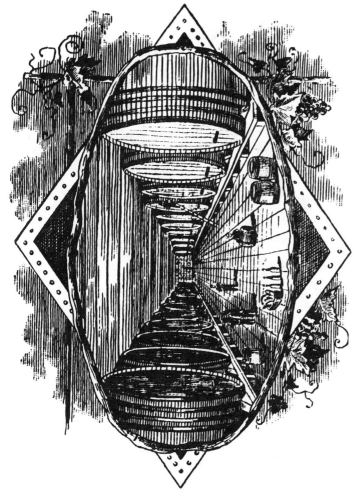

Interior view of the Medoc Vineyards warehouse in 1897 (*courtesy North Carolina Collection, UNC Library, Chapel Hill*)

Charles W. Garrett (*courtesy North Carolina Collection, UNC Library, Chapel Hill*)

was the Arkansas-Texas-Tennessee sector. Paul Garrett professed to being an indifferent salesman, but there can be no doubt that he was a genius in the art of persuading. When the Wrights instructed him in the ways of the old-fashioned drummer and he started on his beat alone in rural Texas, he made his first sale to a reluctant saloon keeper in Blossom Prairie by eloquently describing the vast reaches of a scuppernong vine and the luscious flavor of its grapes, following up with a taste of sample wine from a vial carried in a pocket case. Garrett was delighted not only by the size of the ensuing order but also by the assurance given him that a stripling salesman did not necessarily have to take a shot of whiskey before transacting business with a barkeep.

The Wrights were delighted also when he reported on his first tour and shortly thereafter took him in as a partner in a venture named the Standard Wine Company, bottlers and distributors, and set him up in Little Rock to break the drought of Arkansas temperance laws. Later they moved to Memphis. For a time the business flourished, so well that the plant at Ringwood could not supply wines in sufficient quantities. Accordingly, the junior associate was dispatched to St. Louis for supplies, then to California, where he found no suitable goods in the northern counties but contracted with the San Gabriel Company and others for considerable amounts of fortified wines. Much of the Standard's business involved shipments in tankcar lots from California to customers in and near Texas; smaller orders were filled by direct deliveries from St. Louis or Ringwood. It would seem that the Halifax County concern had dwindled to a minor aspect of its chief salesman's activities and a crescent stream of sweet vintages beckoned them on to fortune. But difficulties ensued, especially when young Paul was married and refused to leave the main office in Memphis for the drab rounds of a traveling salesman.

Before long he sold out to the Wrights and went back to Ringwood, where, by some strange quirk, the manager of his uncle's firm offered him the exclusive sales agency for its entire output. Drawing up his own contract without a lawyer's help, he stipulated that he should pay a flat price not only for all the wines that it made but also for all that it might make or control in the future. His hope was that the plant would enlarge its operations and thus enable him to direct and manage a force of salesmen while he remained with his family at home. After a month's trip on the road and paper profits of four thousand dollars, Garrett was informed by the manager, incidentally his wife's brother married to his own cousin, that the contract was cancelled since he was making more money than did the firm itself. The upshot of the inevitable hassle was a double-barreled family feud and a split. The future "dean of American vintners" would never submit to reduction to the rank of a salaried salesman.

Renting a tiny warehouse not far off in Littleton and collecting his debt in barrels of wine, he set forth again after sales, with his father keeping his books, a little sister putting on shipping tags, and a reliable Negro boy taking care of the shipments. Not surprisingly, the Ringwood Company soon shut off access to its goods, and to fill the orders already booked, he arranged with the Urbana Wine Company of Hammondsport, New York, to forward a few carloads of Catawba and port. In his dictated account of these early days Paul Garrett frankly admitted his determination to provide such competition that he would shortly be asked to rejoin forces with the old family firm. But instead, the breach widened, a law suit for libel cast a long-lingering plague on both houses, and the old Charles W. Garrett and Company lost business to Garrett and Company, as the new firm was called. The choice of the title was indeed a shrewd one, for the family name stood for a well-established concern with a solid reputation for superior goods and reliability in delivering them. Its still scuppernong, as well as its sparkling, was rated among the best of its kind—and the Garrett brandy knew few rivals in the South. Their reputation certainly helped to stave off a decline in sales even as it aided the new firm to ground itself on a substantial basis.

In the later nineteenth century there was always room for more makers of wines of high quality in both the South and the North. The growth of the native population and the newer hordes of immigrants continually added to the numbers of potential customers. California producers saw to it that tariff rates ran up the prices of foreign competitors, even while most of them were content themselves to turn out wines little better than those traditionally sold in bulk at the waterfront in San Francisco. Migration of good southern families to the West and North after the Civil War had carried knowledge of the muscadine wines all over the country. The Gay Nineties fashions encouraged dining out at restaurants and hotels, where birthday dinners called for champagne as almost comme il faut even among those who disliked it. As the cities grew, high society with its wining and dining was even more widely publicized than the likewise-increasing slums. Still another factor in expanding the market was salesmanship and advertising.

As we have seen, Sidney Weller had flourished as nurseryman and vintner by sending out from the back country of Halifax County a multitude

Medoc Vineyards in 1897 (*courtesy North Carolina Collection, UNC Library, Chapel Hill*)

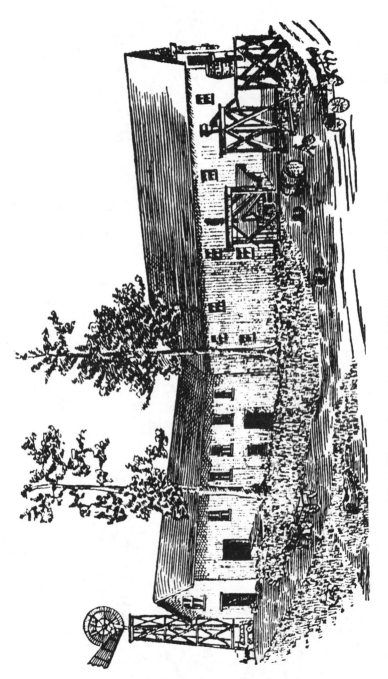

Medoc Vineyards warehouse in 1897 (*courtesy North Carolina Collection, UNC Library, Chapel Hill*)

of letters to agricultural journals or to newspapers. One or the other of the Garretts who succeeded him continued the practice but on a vastly reduced scale. In 1872, for example, a communication simply headed "C. W. Garrett & Co. Ringwood, Halifax County, N.C." informed the readers of *The South* that prospects for growing grapes were good in the region what with land, labor, and the posts for arbors so cheap, and the *Carolina Farmer* [2] among others promptly reprinted it. The venerable *American Agriculturist* * and other northern periodicals occasionally informed their readers about the size and abundant crops of the scuppernongs, especially after a grower like the Garretts sent in a sample of grapes or wine. But both the old and the new firms made comparatively little use of such means. Their dependence was largely on salesmen, on a few paid advertisements plus an occasional folder or booklet, along with exhibits at fairs and expositions. When, as we have seen, in 1905 the federal government began its investigation of muscadines, the Medoc Vineyards figured importantly in the study because many of their scuppernongs were among the oldest in the possession of any commercial establishment, and their collaboration brought favorable attention to the company in the limited circles of pomologists. As the twentieth century advanced C. W. Garrett and Company was more and more overshadowed by the gigantic growth of its rival—and in time Paul Garrett was owner of both.

Before he was able to buy a chief interest in the Medoc, however, much water went over the mill; millions of gallons of wine had to be sold. At the outset Paul Garrett realized that the backbone of his business was the scuppernong and that he could not prosper merely on imports of bulk wines from New York. Accordingly, he had to forage at a distance, since the Ringwood Wine Company was already draining the grape crops from surrounding Halifax County vineyards. In Columbus County he knew "an honorable Connecticut Yankee," as he called him, once an itinerant clock repairman but now settled with some crude wine-making machinery on a small farm near Vineland, as Whiteville was once named. Concluding arrangements with him, Garrett authorized a payment of fifty cents per bushel for the grapes to be processed, despite warnings that such a good price would overwhelm the available facilities with offerings from neighbors. When such indeed proved to be the case and he had rushed back from Ringwood in answer to Rockwell's telegram, "I am

---

*The *Agriculturist* in 1868 noted receipt of grapes from M. T. Garrett and later carried a short article on them, with a picture of the fruit (XXVII [Nov., 1868], 413).

swamped," he found the narrow road leading through the woods to the Yankee's farm blocked with high-wheeled carts and small wagons each loaded with one to three bushels of scuppernongs, and several hundred barrels of the fresh grapes waiting in the yard to be unloaded. Exacting promises from many farmers who had available teams that they would come by Vineland the next day and pick up empty barrels and hogsheads, he wired to Wilmington to have shipped that night some thirty empty molasses hogsheads holding about 160 gallons each and two carloads of empty whiskey barrels. In his words,

All of the morning was spent making plans and readjustments. With the arrival this day of the hogsheads and barrels, and drafting all of the Rockwell family into the work, together with such of the neighbors as we could get together, we would with an ax knock out the poorest heads of the molasses hogsheads (generally having five to ten pounds of sugar in them) and boring a bung-hole near the bottom and covering it with straw, we would grind them full of grapes. Putting an empty tub under the straw-covered bung-hole, we would let the juice drip out, and old Mrs. Rockwell, holding the baby Martha in her arms, would dip out the juice into buckets with a long-handled gourd, and I would pour the juice into the empty whiskey barrels, adding the necessary quantity of sugar to each barrel. This was certainly primitive winemaking. We wasted three fourths of the fresh juice because the pulp would not disintegrate until fermentation had started, but we couldn't wait. What we did save was quality wine, and in due time it helped materially in establishing the reputation of Paul Garrett's Scuppernong.[3]

Primitive winemaking indeed! But, then, in the view of present-day vintners all the old-fashioned ways are primitive. Who now remembers when it was standard to clarify the must by dropping into it the whites of eggs, or even oxblood, before running the whole batch through a woolen blanket?* Near the coast, filters were often made of crushed seashells "wrapped or mixed with clean, bright-broom grass placed in a large funnel."[4]

After the death of his father, followed soon by that of his wife, Garrett moved to Weldon, also in Halifax County, well within the radius of his sources of grapes and strategically situated with respect to transportation. The town was a division terminal of the earliest railroad from Virginia, a canal dating from 1835 had opened traffic from the lower Roanoke River, and the Wilmington and Weldon carried memories of having once

---

*Gerald McCarthy recommended "a good-sized pinch of dry mustard powder" as an aid in keeping a barrel of new wine from spoiling (N.C. Dept. of Agriculture, *Wine-making at Home*, Biennial Report of Commissioner of Agriculture [Raleigh, N.C., 1905], p. 249).

been hailed as "the longest railroad in the world," after the completion of its 161.5 miles in 1840. Garrett's plant was on the aqueduct at a place named Chockoyotte, an Indian word often simplified in local parlance to "Chocolate," just as, not far away, an ancient tavern called the Old Ordinary became "Old Ornery." Associated with him were two brothers-in-law, Dr. Ty Harrison and George Harrison, and a cousin Frank Garrett. For a time he toyed with the idea of turning the business over to them and going off to join Cecil Rhodes in Africa. Instead he made it boom. With funds from his father's estate, credit from banks in Richmond, and loyal help from relatives and sundry other Tarheel associates, Garrett and Company soon outgrew its premises. Despite the Panic of 1893 and amidst the bankers' fears that Bryan and the Silverites would win the election of 1896, he was able to obtain funds for the construction of a new warehouse, to which he was soon forced to add wings. When what he called his "expanding spree" dominated his decisions, his gambles were matched only by the renewed efforts he put forth. At the time a national depression stalled commerce all over the nation a Weldon paper proudly noted: "Messrs. Garrett & Co. have shipped over 3000 gallons of home made wine in a single shipment one day last week. Can any place in the South beat that?"[5] The next year when a telephone line was strung up to connect Garrett's office in town with his new plant at Chockoyotte, the paper observed that the winery was not only one of the largest in the region, its wares sold from Maine to California, but its owner was a "level headed business man" with "push and energy enough in him for any ten men."[6] After moving to Weldon, Garrett recalled during his last days, "I realized that any hope of renewed association with my uncle's firm, then operating under the name of the Medoc Vineyards Company, was not to be entertained, so I felt my first real necessity of enlarged operations by accumulating larger inventories of goods, always one of my hobbies—which has stood me in good stead."[7]

There is of course no single clue to a man's character, but something of Garrett's amazing drive may be glimpsed in his phrases like "one of my hobbies" or "my expanding sprees." Business was a game to be played, the risks many, the rewards, ultimately in millions, a secondary result of riding a hobby or, perhaps appropriately enough for a vintner, going on a "spree." How shrewdly he could play the game is illustrated in his bid for the contract to supply the state of South Carolina with wines for its liquor stores. In the Democratic primary of 1892 the reformers in that state had persuaded the authorities to place a separate box at each polling place so that public opinion might be ascertained on the question of state-wide prohibition. When a great majority voted in favor of the proposal and an ensuing stringent bill was in the legislative hopper, the Populist governor, Benjamin Tillman, engineered the substitution of a state monopoly to go into effect the next year. The profits of the retail stores were to be evenly divided between counties and municipalities and those derived from the state's handling of the liquors were to go into its treasury. A capable businessman, husband of an outstanding officer of the Woman's Christian Temperance Union, was appointed to head the project—and was promptly expelled from his Baptist congregation. This was the least of his troubles, for in a few months rioting broke out in Darlington and elsewhere, the militia called out by Tillman refused to "foster civil war among the brethren," as its general in Charleston put it, and a "Dispensary War" was on. The governor, a poor white by background, eventually restored order with the help of rednecks from his rural strongholds, but the subsequent graft by the state commissioners soon soured America's first attempt at state control through the dispensary system.[8]

Proceeding to Columbia when only a one-story wooden building housed the bottling works, Garrett noticed the array of whiskey barrels, their heads smashed in with axes, and unwashed bottles gurgling as they were thrust down into their contents. While he waited for the governor to return from commencement exercises at Clemson he helped out by placing orders for the manager with producers of handbottling equipment. When Tillman arrived he displayed a remarkable grasp of the liquor business but insisted that his state would purchase only in bulk. When Garrett was allowed a major part and not the whole order for wines, and subsequent trips netted disgustingly smaller returns, he lost interest, until a bottle salesman tipped him off that the commissioners were in a quandary over the poor sale of wines and ready to consider buying them already bottled. After he secured a written invitation to attend a meeting of these gentry, he was forced to refuse their blunt request for a ten percent kickback but managed to get them to listen to his explanation of why their wine sales were disappointing and to his promises that he would not only guarantee a profit to the state but would take away any unsalable goods. Acceptance of his proposals was later clinched when he shrewdly remarked to an influential commissioner that a day might come when it would be handy to have one dealer who could swear he had never paid them a cent.

His arrangements with the business director involved permission for him or his agent to visit each of the 120 liquor stores in South Carolina, to show the local managers how to display and handle wines. And he himself took on the first trial in Columbia, after having shipped five carloads, one for each of the five dispensaries there.

I shall never forget the consternation [he dictated] when my first truckload of about 300 cases backed up to one of the largest dispensaries in Columbia and the manager flatly refused to let it come into the place, stating that he would never account for that much wine in ten years and that the work put on him to keep account of that much wine was too much, and he just couldn't do it—that he would quit his job first. I finally persuaded him to let the goods be unloaded and I started to work. I ordered his Negro workers to bring in several buckets of clean water, and, rolling up my sleeves, and with a rag, I got into one of the big windows and started washing it. Remonstrances flew quick and fast—that it was against the law to put any goods on display in a show window—but I kept steadily at work and out-talked him, and soon I had a most unusual display of wine in the window.

Just after I had finished . . . along came a carriage with two elegantly dressed ladies out for their evening ride, and seeing the wine display in the dispensary window they had the driver stop the carriage. After admiring the unusual display for a few minutes they turned and walked into the dispensary. These ladies happened to be of Columbia's most exclusive aristocracy, and such a thing as a lady going into a dispensary had never been dreamed of. The manager and two of his clerks were very courteous and the ladies purchased half a dozen bottles of wine—and the ice was broken. . . . I held this business with the dispensary system almost as a monopoly until its dissolution.[9]*

Garrett and Company won a medal for its blackberry and scuppernong exhibited in 1900 at the Paris Exposition, but in 1904 the Big White Grape scored a greater triumph, for Paul Garrett's Special Champagne, made entirely from its delectable juice, was awarded the grand prize for sparkling wines at the Louisiana Purchase Exposition held in St. Louis. The significance of this honor is enhanced by the distinguished nature of the competition, for wines from the Hammondsport vicinity of New York, the Great Lakes area, and the state of California (including some from Paul Masson) were displayed along with those from ten growers in Argentina, fifty in Italy, and several hundred in France.[10] And St. Louis itself was a famous wine center, original home of Cook's Imperial Champagne, one of the most celebrated vintages of the nation.†

*South Carolina's state system was abolished in 1907, and the county stores substituted for it closed with the advent of state-wide prohibition in 1915.

†The cellar of the American Wine Company which produced it at the time is still extant. During World War II a winery with the same name in the city was secretly owned by Hitler's henchman Joachim von Ribbentrop, an ex-champagne salesman (Adams, p. 179).

Riding the wave of celebrity stimulated by this signal honor, Garrett made a bid for further recognition among the carriage trade by issuing in 1905 a tastefully designed booklet printed on the expensive stock common to dance programs of the period and entitled *The Art of Serving Wine*. It might properly have borne a subtitle: "Including the Art of Selling It."[11] The place of publication is given as Norfolk, Virginia, whither he had only recently shifted headquarters from Weldon; and St. Louis and San Francisco appeared in smaller type. After the usual advice as to how, when, and what kinds of wines should be used, the "etiquette of the glass," and persuasive arguments that wine is a real food, a health-giving joy, as well as a cure for the "liquor evil," a description of the scuppernong grape is presented along with the story of its connections with Roanoke Island, fortified by a cut of the "Old Mother Scuppernong Vine" itself. The wine is declared to be unique in that it was not pressed from the grapes but allowed to free its juice under its own pressure after they had been "ground." To give it a romantic history, Garrett offers a synopsis of a "beautiful Indian legend" calculated to account for a reddish color which certain "scuppernongs" disclose. The Indian legend is based on a long poem imitative of Longfellow and called *The White Doe: The Fate of Virginia Dare*.[12] The author was Sallie Southall Cotten, a young club woman married to a genteel Carolinian. It is well illustrated with cuts of John White's celebrated drawings of Roanoke Indians and photographs of scuppernongs growing on trellises in a "Virginia Dare vineyard" near Manteo.

Mrs. Cotten's book contains as a prefatory essay a history of the early interest in the grapes of the island. Garrett used his booklet to advertise *The White Doe* and offered to send free copies of the poem upon payment of ten cents for postage. Less romantic but by no means lacking in imagination is the section of the booklet pertaining to Garrett's wines.[13] He begins with Virginia Dare, described as a "Tokay Type," product of the "White Scuppernong," with "no equal as a wine grape." Its flavor is described as follows: "Of a moderate sweetness yet preserving in all its natural character the original acidity and unequalled aroma of the grape, this wine will be found not only deliciously fruity, but with just enough bite and tartness to make it appetizing and refreshing, and with its natural acids a great aid to digestion." Such is its creator's original conception of the famed beverage that he named and within a few years made the most popular vinous drink of the United States.

Next in order came his Minnehaha, "dry, not sweet" and likewise made from pure juice of the "White Scuppernong." It might be likened, the booklet suggests, to a "Haut Sauterne or a superior Rhine Wine," but only in a very general way. Third comes Pocahontas, "a Light Port Type"—in reality a "Red Virginia Dare," which retains the "natural fruit acids" lacking in "the ordinary Port." Next in order is Paul Garrett's Special Champagne, intended to be unsurpassed by any rival "foreign or domestic." In explaining why it cost such a good round sum the process of making it is outlined in considerable detail. "Test the wine," Garrett advised, "not the label"—and he offered to replace "with any imported brand" every bottle of his Special that proved unsatisfactory. A second and cheaper line of champagne was his Southern Sunshine, not quite so dry, free from artificial flavors or "other sources of headache," but "finished in a shorter time."

Garrett's F.F.V. Claret, made from Norton's Virginia Seedling and Ives grapes, is given less space, as is the case also with his Old North State Blackberry, port, sherry, and strawberry. He offered port "from three to twenty-five years old, and sherry dating from the 1870s." Of the strawberry, he observed, "we have put up annually a few thousand gallons" but "we have never pushed the sale of this." His remarks on Altar or Sacramental Wine include a promise to furnish it to impecunious parishes free of charge if "any member of the clergy" applied for it and the costs of container and transportation were supplied by the consignee. All his wines were sold in case lots in bottles bearing his name and trademark blown in the glass. His trademark carried a picture of an eagle, wings outstretched, hovering over a cluster of scuppernongs bordered by Confederate battle flags and bearing the words "Garrett's American Wines." The art work is quite pleasing. On a page headed "How to Order," Garrett mentioned "all the leading wine merchants" as sources but noted that the rational place to buy his wines would be at the grocer's. "Inconsistent legislation," however, rendered this impossible in many cases; hence druggists, he announced, were apt to be more likely suppliers. Or orders could be directly addressed to the home plant in Norfolk.

In addition to pictures of his medals and the ribbon from the St. Louis Exposition the booklet carries at the end a batch of recipes, principally of fruit punches but also of Garrett's "Sky Ball" (Pocahontas and seltzer) and "Paul and Virginia"—this last consisting of a half glass of Virginia Dare and a similar portion of Paul Garrett's Special. The Big White Grape had now reached the acme of American alcoholic success; it had been elevated to the stature of an ingredient in highballs. One passes reluctantly the formula for "Minnehaha and White Rock" in favor of that for "Roanoke Punch," a concoction to which the scuppernong might be expected to be well adapted. Here it is: "Juice of 10 lemons strained, juice of 8 oranges strained, 1 pineapple cut in pieces, 2 quarts of F.F.V. Claret, 2 quarts Virginia Dare, 2 quarts Pocahontas, 1 gallon cold tea. Let stand on ice four hours. Serve in punch glasses with cake." It was a good recipe, as certain dear old ladies may still remember—potent, too.

The Art of Serving Wine was undoubtedly a success. The romantic appeal to history in backing his scuppernong with ancestry and tradition fitted in perfectly with the vogue for sentimental historical novels regnant around the turn of the century, like *To Have and to Hold*, *When Knighthood Was in Flower*, or *Alice of Old Vincennes*, which gave their publishers the first big bite of the best-seller pie. The muted but reiterated suggestions of the purity of his "American Wines" and their freedom from admixture were attuned to the heightened fervor that led in 1906 to the first national legislation on pure foods. The overt reminder of medical values and the stress on light alcoholic content tended to disarm abstainers, and the offer of free altar wines to "those parishes where the matter of expense is of the greatest moment," as the word *poor* was genteelly avoided, might even warrant an occasional "God bless you!" The spirit of "Madison Avenue" was awake in the land—long before the term was invented.

"When Wartime Prohibition began in 1919," says the chief historian of American wines, Garrett "had seventeen plants processing grape juice or wine in North Carolina, Virginia, Ohio, Missouri, New York, and California, with a total capacity of ten million gallons," and he became a billionaire selling wine with the scuppernong flavor.[14] He never really made a billion, but, as it has been well put by someone who knows, "he did pretty well." So did the Big White Grape.

CHAPTER IV

Prohibition

Commercial manufacture of wines in the United States burgeoned during the two decades prior to the enactment of the Volstead Act in 1919. In 1900 about twenty-four million gallons were officially recorded, and roughly thirty-nine in 1918. In volume, California, beginning in the 1880s, surpassed the rest of the country combined, and the percentage coming from the eastern states continued to diminish.[1] Outside of California, grapes used for wine and brandy were estimated at 118,000 tons in 1899 and declined to 80,000 in 1909 and to 64,000 in 1917.[2] The Big White Grape assuredly was bucking the trend, for, as we have seen, the wineries in the South were demanding far more muscadines than growers could supply. Paul Garrett's business likewise bucked the trend, and soon the orders for his "American Wines" pouring in from all over the nation overtaxed facilities at Weldon even after the new building there had been expanded. Of necessity the popular Virginia Dare would become a blend, eventually with only enough of the original grape to tincture the flavor and give it a typical bouquet. And Garrett's company made its first move northward.

Retaining the plant at Weldon, Paul Garrett in 1903 transferred headquarters to Berkley, Virginia, then a newly industrialized municipality with a few textile factories. From his property at the foot of Liberty Street a few minutes' ride by ferry brought one either to Portsmouth or to Norfolk, in which city the community was soon to be absorbed. Railroads fanned out from the center, and steamers and bay boats crowded the harbor, affording quick transportation for seafood and the vegetables and fruits from a vast trucking region. The Edenton-Elizabeth City sector of North Carolina was a finger on the city's outstretched hand. From thousands of farms in Virginia and North Carolina, barrels of fresh grapes and crates of berries were soon on their way to his new plant. To it also bulk wines from California or from the Finger Lakes district of New York were readily moved. Norfolk was a cigar center and a beer producer, and it supported well-established factories dealing in crates and cooperage, one of them turning out more than a thousand barrels a day.[3] The liquor dealers of the Old Dominion in annual conclave spent the morning of October 19, 1906, admiring the large concrete building and splendid equipment at Berkley. The new headquarters were admirably situated for a scuppernong winery. But Garrett's move was also prompted by what he called "the growing prohibition sentiment."

Planters of the Old South like his ancestors in Edgecombe County had never balked at legislation designed to prevent the sale of liquor to slaves, and a jokester might say that long after slavery was gone it was still for the benefit of the blacks that, as Will Rogers quipped, many folks staggered to the polls to vote dry. In 1908 Clarence Poe, assigning reasons for the growth of Prohibition in the South, specified the lack of a large foreign population, the predominance of church influences, and the necessity of keeping liquor from Negroes of the baser sort.[4] Most social historians agree that peace societies and temperance organizations were exceptions to the rule that the "peculiar institution" of the Southland put a damper on the manifold reforms heating the nation during the "Fabulous Forties," a time when, Emerson jocularly observed, everyone in New England was running about with a scheme for bettering the world tucked in his vestpocket. Within six years after the American Temperance Society was organized in Boston, in 1826, there were thirty-one auxiliaries in North Carolina, a majority near Fayetteville, where as early as 1815 the first known temperance organization in the state emerged from an assemblage of Presbyterians.[5] And as soon as it was apparent that Yankee zealots meant to do in slavery as well as alcohol, the South went on its way more independently, with societies, ladies' auxiliaries, parades, sermons, tracts, and in time laws, galore. A second and a third generation enacted replays of the lively tragi-comedy of agitation, with different actors, to be sure, but many more of them—and bigger audiences too. The original motif of personal temperance was harmonized with a second theme of "Do away with the saloons," and both refrains were fused in a swelling chorus shouted with messianic fervor, "Vote Dry." The masters of contention and keepers of the social conscience, both in and out of the churches, called upon the politicians to become their brothers' guardians. The Anti-Saloon League demonstrated how the wisdom of the serpent could be turned against the bite of the adder.

While attempts to dry out the whole state by legislative enactment had been made prior to the Civil War and the principle of local option in chartered towns had been established, apart from a temporary ban on distilling as a war measure, it was not until the present century that the crusaders scored fuller success in North Carolina. In 1903 the rural districts were dried, and five years later came a triumph evident in the maps taken from the Anti-Saloon League's yearbook facing page 62.[6]

But, alas, human experience is always a jump or two ahead of laws, even when legislators are earnestly bent on catching up. The league's summary of the history of subsequent legislation in Carolina, made in its yearbook for 1920, proves the point:

North Carolina is not only under National Prohibition but is also under state statutory Prohibition, the state law having been adopted by a referendum on May 26, 1908, the vote being 113,612 for Prohibition and 69,416 against Prohibition. This law prohibited not only the sale but the manufacture of intoxicating liquors and became operative January 1, 1909.

The legislature of 1911, by an almost unanimous vote in both Houses, passed a Prohibition law (known as the near-beer law) prohibiting "the sale of near-beer, beerine and other similar drinks, containing alcohol, cocaine, morphine or other opium derivative," except in certain cases. The Legislature also passed a law forbidding clubs to maintain "a club room or other place where intoxicating liquors are received, kept or stored for barter, sale, exchange, distribution or division among the members of any such club, or association or aggregation of persons, or to or among any other person or persons by any means whatever."

The General Assembly of 1913 passed a strong search and seizure law making over one gallon of liquor in one's possession prima facie evidence of guilt.

The General Assembly of 1915 passed an act to prohibit the delivery and receipt of more than one quart of liquor in 15 days, whether for personal use or otherwise.

The General Assembly of 1917 passed a bill making the manufacture of intoxicating liquors a felony and placing the punishment at the minimum of 12 months' imprisonment in state's prison.

After July 1, 1917, the state became bone dry territory, and no liquor advertisements were allowed to circulate through the mails.

It is probable that the Anti-Saloon League will ask the next General Assembly for legislation to carry into effect, so far as this commonwealth is concerned, the Eighteenth Amendment to the Federal constitution. The state laws do not prohibit the manufacture and sale of wines and ciders.

The illicit manufacture of liquor in the mountains of North Carolina presents a serious problem. "Moonshine" liquor sells at retail for from $10 to $30 per quart [*sic*]. But the sentiment against it is very pronounced and the state and Federal authorities are gradually creating better conditions.

The North Carolina General Assembly of 1919 ratified the Prohibition Amendment to the Federal Constitution, the Senate voting unanimously without a roll call (49 out of 50 being present) on January 10, 1919, and the House voting 93 to 10 (17 members being absent or not voting) on January 14. North Carolina was the twenty-eighth state to ratify.[7]

Behind each of the measures recorded by the league lay causative factors not easily coped with. For example, the law passed in 1915 cut down the legal ration to one quart of liquor every fifteen days. Back of it was the considerable amount of booze legally flowing into the state presumably for personal use but much of it destined for blind-tiger drug stores. In 1914 it was disclosed that one druggist in Raleigh within three months had filled 3,990 prescriptions for whiskey, 555 for beer, twenty-six for gin, fifty for wine, and fourteen for brandy. Another druggist had received 835 gallons of spirits in a five-month period.[8] (Just a year earlier Bishop John C. Kilgo had declared in full confidence, "Prohibition is a great success.") When the rationing began to demonstrate effects, bootleggers rushed in supplies from Washington in automobiles, and blockaders helped to fill the void with local products. In 1919 the Collector of Internal Revenue for the eastern counties declared: "We have more illicit distilleries than any state in the Union or any other portion of the earth, and the number is increasing."[9] In 1920 of all the stills seized by Federal agents more than one fifth were captured in North Carolina.[10] No one apparently was stunned. It was an old story.* During the years 1877–81 illicit stills seized by the officers numbered 4,061, with 7,000 Tarheels arrested, twenty-six agents killed, and fifty-six wounded.[11]

While the percentage of moonshining among sand lappers and swamp angels in the coastal counties also ran high, there is strong likelihood that the classic locale for the practice of the art in the South was the upcountry region. Revenue officers lifted their eyes unto the hills as a regular routine. Moreover, the expression *mountain dew* is almost an affectionate metonym for whiskey in Dixie. Scottish forebears may have had something to do with the incipient vogue of this term, for one of its early meanings is *scotch whisky*. Toward the end of the nineteenth century mountain dew derived sanction in Carolina also from a Winston firm incorporated in the state and called the Casper Company, self-proclaimed "the largest mail order whiskey house." It featured in its advertising and proudly blazoned on its labels MOUNTAIN DEW, pure corn whiskey, eight years old and selling for $2.25 a gallon. A gallon! *Eheu Fugaces*! A cheaper grade, called Wild Cat, was also available, at $1.10; and among its wines was Pure North Carolina Scuppernong Sweet, 85 cents per gallon. The instructions for ordering are not without interest: "You can only receive whiskey secretly by express"; if sent by freight, which was cheaper, it had to be marked "Whiskey." And customers desiring a bit

---

*In 1875 the N.C. State Fair offered a diploma for the best copper still "with worm attached" exhibited by a state maker.

more secrecy might also "make remittance to the Minston M'f'g. Co. . . . and these people will turn the same over to us immediately."[12]

Another advertisement may be inserted here as an illustration of a standard medical device. It also invokes the dew of the mountains. Chiefly it attests the merits of the Old Nick Whiskey Company of Panther Creek. At first glance the name may appear to be a figment of the humorous imagination, like Happy Hooligan or perhaps Demon Rum itself—but not so. Panther Creek is one of ten places so named in North Carolina, and both the Wachovia and the First National banks are mentioned as references. The formula for Old Nick stemmed from a revered patriot of Revolutionary War fame, Colonel Joseph Williams, whose son Nicholas continued to carry on a business started shortly after 1765 on the family acres, located originally on the frontier in Surry County and now in Forsyth. When the law forbidding distilleries outside of chartered towns was enacted in 1903 the legislature promptly incorporated the Williams' place as Williams, N.C. In 1908 with the passage of a stricter Prohibition act Williams perforce reverted to a mere farm, and the boss moved his stills and some of his several hundred employees off to Kentucky. The homespun appeal of the Old Nick Company begins in apostolic style:

Men and brethren, stop *now* the use of these Northern and Western *adulterated* whiskies before you injure yourself and family for *life*, furnish your good wife with something pure and harmless for her cough, cold, weakness and loss of appetite. She needs it, she deserves it, and if you are a good husband, you will get it, and thereby not only improve her health and that of the children who sometimes get on the puny list, but will save some Doctor bills as "Old Nick" (as pure as the mountain dew where it is made) is good for coughs, colds, chills, loss of appetite, indisposition and malaria; and those suffering with *weak lungs* can find nothing of more benefit than some of the genuine "Old Nick" Rye Whiskey.[13]

Nothing less than three gallons was to be shipped. Old Nick appears to have held a record for length of service to the health of the community. No Kentucky rival is known to have lasted so long.[14] It is exceptional also in having been made legally.

Competing with regular spirits as therapeutic beverages were of course a multitude of patent remedies, among them the following (their alcoholic percentages in parentheses): Peruna (28.5), Lydia Pinkham's Vegetable Compound (20.6), Baker's Stomach Bitters (42.6), Hooker's Wigwam Tonic (20.7), and quite a variety of sarsaparillas of high potency. A nostrum called Whiskol (28.2) was advertised as a "non-intoxicating stimulant."[15]

While reactions to the sumptuary legislation were pretty much the same wherever state or local laws sought to enforce abstinence, and there was general complaint that Prohibition did not prohibit, sentiment in favor of intervention by federal authority gathered momentum. Congress made it illegal to ship liquor into territory forbidding manufacture or sale (effective date: July 1, 1917). Declaration of war against Germany brought on restrictions on the production of alcoholic beverages as a war measure, and soon thereafter the ratification of the Eighteenth Amendment to the Constitution was quickly followed up by the enabling Volstead Act, passed over President Wilson's veto in the fall of 1919. In January, 1920, the Great Experiment began. Wayne B. Wheeler, chief counsel and lobbyist of the Anti-Saloon League, was immortalized in verse:

> Many drops of water,
> Many grains of sand
> Make the whole damn' nation
> Wayne B. Wheeler-land.

Nightclub actors performed mock-funeral ceremonies for John Barleycorn, and Tin Pan Alley tuned up with a doleful ditty beginning, "How sad and still tonight / On the banks of the old distillery. / The cobwebs cob in the old machinery." On January 16, 1920, less than an hour after the deadline set by national law, six masked hoodlums drove a truck into a Chicago freight yard, herded the trainmen into a shanty, and made off with the whiskey in two boxcars. [16] And less than a decade later the assistant attorney general in charge of enforcement frankly declared: "There may be, and probably there is, more illicit distilling now than before prohibition . . . but the still problem is a comparatively unimportant phase of lawlessness at the present time." [17] In North Carolina, in the final year of national Prohibition federal agents seized 1,330 stills and hauled 1,417 individuals off to jails. [18] Yet, even as the lawbreaking went merrily on, the propaganda of the Prohibitionists in the state continued to be effective politically, for a straw vote conducted by the *Literary Digest* in 1932 showed North Carolina and Kansas as the only two states a majority of whose voters were willing to continue the Eighteenth Amendment in force. [19] Evidently, Tarheels did not heed the injunction of Senator Buncombe Bob Reynolds: "Vote the way you drink."

Although wine was far less a target than beer or whiskey for the arrows of reformers and sometimes seems to have been all but forgotten in the legal shuffling betwixt Wets and Drys, the Bible Belt, as Henry Mencken liked to call the southern states, was after 1900 an increasingly unpromising province for those who pressed the grape. In Carolina the so-called Watts Law of 1903, granting local option to incorporated towns only, exempted wines and ciders as well as fruit and grape brandies when sold in quantities of five gallons or more. Evidently the wineries were to be protected. In 1908 it was stipulated that wines could be sold only when sales were effected at the place of manufacture and the goods sealed in containers of no less than two and a half gallons. In 1913 the Search and Seizure Law confined sales to drug stores or medical repositories and forbade anyone to have more than three gallons of wine in his possession. Paul Garrett was wise in moving out of the state before the jaws tightened. But his most essential grapes were supplied largely from Carolina. It was awkward to have to rush tank cars loaded with expensive scuppernong juice from the press-houses at Weldon or Aberdeen to the plant at Norfolk before fermentation made them subject to seizure, but it was done. It was a joy to note the escalating sales of Virginia Dare and other wines based on the muscadines, but there was also a constant worry over a shortage of supplies of their precious juice even when "pure scuppernong" was blended with bulk wines from California or New York. By 1915 "few large wine cellars in the East" failed to use some California wine for blending.*

Garrett encouraged southern nurserymen and vineyardists to increase production of muscadines. At the same time, as we have seen, the fresh fruit business was booming. One of the many growers whose grapes he promised to buy was the Southern Vineyard Company, with headquarters at Sandy Cross, N.C. This firm, in cooperation with the North Carolina Fruit and Truck Company, attempted a cooperative venture in Perquimans and Gates counties in 1905. Their promotion pamphlet states that for $350 per acre, payable in installments, the company would plant scuppernongs and James grapes for purchasers, taking care of the vines and selling the harvest on shares. "To eliminate all elements of risk to an investor, Garrett & Co. of Norfolk, Va. have contracted to take all the grapes at 75 cents per bushel for the first five hundred acres sold of this

---

*Hiram S. Dewey, president of the American Wine Growers' Association, so declared at the first meeting of the International Congress of Viticulture in the U. S. A. (*Official Report of a Session of the International Congress of Viticulture* [San Francisco, 1915], p. 301).

cooperative vineyard." A further assurance is given that Garrett and Co. "have an immense trade and are rated very high in Dunn and Brad-street."[20]*

By 1908, with a stricter law passed and the lingering smaller wineries rapidly disappearing, it must have been difficult to persuade a farmer to plant more vines, unless he had his eye solely on the fresh fruit market. And in Virginia, the last of the southern states to go dry, pressures were likewise building up as Richmond's doughty Bishop Cannon and his clever cohorts of the Anti-Saloon League pulled the political levers. All over the eastern grape areas even larger wineries closed shop when laws barred them from selling their wares locally and the cheap prices of California rivals menaced profits. Selling off some of his Virginia holdings, Paul Garrett in 1912 once again moved his headquarters, this time to Penn Yan, in the Finger Lakes district of New York, a noted eastern bastion of table wines and champagnes. His activities during the Great National Drought will be treated in a subsequent chapter.

Meanwhile, for the effects of national Prohibition on wines and grapes in general we may resort to the neat summary presented by Leon D. Adams in his admirable survey *The Wines of America*:

What happened next was totally unexpected. At first, the gloomy winegrowers began ripping out their vineyards, but soon they were wishing they hadn't. For the Drys had overlooked, or else failed to understand, an obscure provision of the Volstead Act—Section 29, which dealt with the home production of fruit juices. Originally placed in the law to placate the Virginia apple farmers, Section 29 permitted a householder to make "nonintoxicating cider and fruit juices exclusively for use in his home" to the extent of 200 gallons yearly. In 1920 began the peddling of "juice grapes" to home winemakers and bootleggers from pushcarts in New York and from trucks in Boston and other cities. Suddenly, grape prices at the vineyards leaped from ten dollars a ton to the unheard-of figure of one hundred dollars, and this started a feverish new rush of vine-planting across the nation. Soon more "nonintoxicating" wine was being made in America's basements each year than the commercial wineries had ever made before. Prohibition had brought the growers a bonanza.

---

*Testimonials on the muscadines appear in letters from George C. Husmann, famed pomologist, W. F. Massey, North Carolina horticulturist, Ollen E. Warren, prominent nurseryman of Greenville, R. R. Bulluck of Ringwood, and Mrs. Cornelius James of Parmele, growers. Among the illustrations in the pamphlet is a cut of an ancient scuppernong, a variety whose crop "never has been a failure" in Eastern North Carolina (p. 19).

In 1870 the Southern Land Company promoted a cooperative emigration from New England for settlement at Hyde Park in Hyde County. Plots of 20 acres each were offered at $100 each and the "Scuppernong Grape" was featured as one of the economic attractions. A copy of the company's leaflet *North Carolina: The Garden Spot of the World* . . . (n.pl. [1870]) is in the Hyde County folder in the manuscript collection in Duke University Library.

The California grape growers, grown wealthy overnight, had only one gripe—a shortage of refrigerator cars—which they bitterly blamed on the railroads. Prosperity in the vineyard areas lasted exactly five years. Then, in 1925, the beleaguered railroads obliged by abruptly ending the car shortage. With plenty of refrigerator cars, too much fruit was shipped, and when it rotted at the eastern terminals waiting for buyers who already had enough, the bottom dropped out of the grape market. From the collapse in 1925, except during the Second World War, California suffered from a chronic surplus of grapes until 1971.

More than a hundred wineries in California and New York and some dozens in New Jersey, Ohio, and Missouri survived the dry laws. Throughout Prohibition, they legally made sacramental wines and champagnes for the clergy, medicinal wines for sale by druggists on doctors' prescriptions, salted wines for cooking (salted to make them undrinkable), and grape juice both fresh and condensed as a concentrate. Medicinal wine tonic became a popular tipple, because buyers soon learned its secret; when refrigerated, the horrible-tasting medicaments settled to the bottom of the bottle, leaving a drinkable wine. Of the sacramental wines, the greatest volume was sold through rabbis, because the Jewish faith requires the religious use of wine in the home. Anybody could call himself a rabbi and get a permit to buy wine legally, merely by presenting a list of his congregation. Millions of all faiths and of no faith became members of fake synagogues, some without their knowledge when the lists were copied from telephone directories. (My next-door neighbor in San Francisco bought port and sherry at four dollars a gallon from a rabbi whose synagogue was a hall bedroom, which he called "Congregation L'Chayim.")[21]

It may be interjected at this point that abuse of sacramental wine was one alcoholic sin of which North Carolina was virtually guiltless. In 1922, for example, only 406.73 gallons were shipped from bonded warehouses in the state for religious purposes; in 1933 the figure was 724.91.* For New York the similar wine in 1922 was registered at 597,000 gallons and dropped to 416,000 in 1933.[22] So great was worship in the Empire State with its motto *Excelsior*.

Studies of the economic effects of national Prohibition show that after a year or so of diminished activity, production of wines registered an enormous increase, furthered in 1925–26 by the sharp drops in the prices of California grapes and checked to a degree in 1929 with the onset of the Great Depression.[23] For the period 1929–30 seventy-five percent of the wine then consumed is believed to have been made in homes, in contrast with fifty percent of the beer and twenty-five of the spirits.[24] The range of the ingredients was considerable, from fresh corn and dandelion blossoms to raisins and rhubarb. Even the breakfast prunes supplied to pris-

---

*Still wines in bond in North Carolina in 1933 amounted to 541 gallons only—all Concord.

oners in Sing Sing were levied upon, and the warden had to hire a private detective to identify those of his inmates who worked vinous wonders with them.[25] As we have seen, during the dry era 1920–33 more wine—or what passed as such—was made in the United States than had been turned out by all the commercial wineries during the several years preceding.

North Carolina, however, may not have been typical. It had no large cities with foreigners making the basements of tenement houses reek with the effluvia of fermenting must. In Charlotte the going price quoted in July, 1930, for "domestic" wine was a dollar per quart, and that of non-"imported" spirits ranged from $1.25 to $4.00 for the same amount.[26] There was thus little incentive to become a "wino," with copious local supplies of more ardent spirits readily available at reasonable prices and such celebrated products as Craven County Corn or East Lake Rye competing. One needed to discriminate, to be sure, especially among the offerings available only in half-gallon jars. Shake the contents well and examine the "bead"—that was to test for potency. Unscrew the zinc lid and take a sniff or a snifter—that was to detect the percentage of fusel oil, or if one's expertise was sufficiently advanced, to ascertain whether "bug-juice" had become an ingredient as a result of failure to screen the mash from insects. Dried applies or peaches helped to promote potability. When the magazine *Fortune* reported on the "U. S. Liquor Industry" in the fall of 1931, its editors estimated 24,990 stills for North Carolina, surpassed in the South Atlantic region only by Georgia, which had the benefit of Atlanta.[27] According to the Treasury Department's report on alcoholic beverages for 1933, along with the 1330 North Carolina stills seized for the year, 26,000 gallons of spirits and 826,000 gallons of mash were destroyed but only nine gallons of wine were captured. Bootlegging of wine, obviously, was negligible.

There can be no doubt, however, that the percentage of wine makers rose among those Tarheels who ranged the woods for blackberries or muscadines or flailed the scuppernongs from the overhead trellises near their houses. All over the nation many of the home vintners were "good folks," of the kind T. S. Eliot described as "decent"—"their field where a thousand golf balls lie." Professionals were a rarity, like an old Frenchman at Castle Hayne, nicknamed the Bishop and famed in certain quarters for his strawberry vermouth. And even the Bishop fell from grace when one of his customers found a well-preserved little frog at the bottom of one of the brown demijohns in which he dispensed his wares. In academic circles colleagues whose researches were carried on in chemical laboratories were cherished during Prohibition as never before, and some among them discovered anew the virtues of sparkling scuppernong. "Make your wine after a favorite formula and when it is ripened sufficiently insert a piece of 'dry ice' the size of a pea in a chilled bottle of it exactly one half hour before drinking; restore the cork tightly, and behold—champagne." Such was the advice of the wizards of the test tubes. Of course toasts had to be cut short at a birthday party, else the effervescence bubbling in the glass too quickly went the way of all carbon dioxide.

Among the gentry of the Romance language departments, where winemaking was conventionally viewed through rosy-hued French spectacles, there were occasional grape-pressing parties at which the elect among the guests were allowed to trample the grapes. The vintage resultant from one such festival celebrated in a backyard in Durham was actually so good as to command the admiration of Count Sforza, who sipped the scuppernong at a dinner party a year afterward. But perhaps the encomiums evoked from the Italian statesman would have been more restrained if the juice rescued from the washtubs had not been turned over to the superintendency of a German cook trained in the art of making currant wine at Coblenz.

But the buffetings of the Prohibition years took their toll of the grapes of North Carolina even though the gaiety of Tarheels was not utterly suppressed. The following figures (in thousands) from the Census Bureau's reports tell the tale:[28]

	Vines of bearing age				Vines not of bearing age			
	1910	1920	1930	1935	1910	1920	1930	1935
North Carolina	411	544	383	475	120	115	89	81
California	144,098	153,195	242,079	226,498	39,526	21,389	15,762	12,210

Not counted were the isolated vines near dwellings, fairly consequential in the case of muscadines. The accompanying statistics for California suggest the overwhelming dominance of that state in American grape growing. Discounting the fact that raisins and table grapes accounted for a very considerable element in California production at the time, it may seem incredible that the Big White Grape, which constituted perhaps half of North Carolina's commercial vines in 1919, could have survived the competition. The figures help also to explain why Tarheels often found it handier to make their Prohibition tipple out of California-grown

Alicante Bouschets rather than from their own scuppernongs, far superior for making wines though the latter assuredly are.*

In philosophizing over the general residue left from the era of the "experiment noble in purpose," as Herbert Hoover carefully phrased it, a cynic might say that Prohibition gave the Solid South a real bone for internecine political contention. A semanticist might reasonably argue that it enlarged the American vocabulary. The old-fashioned word *saloon* borders on the discard as the transition from *speakeasy* to *night club* and *cocktail bar* might suggest. The term *scofflaw*, however, loiters palely in the shade of *mob*, *take for a ride*, or *highjack*, even though it won a prize offered in 1923 for a term to apply to "the lawless drinker to stab awake his conscience."[29] Will Al Capone and his ilk supplant Robin Hood as a "matter of Romance" for pulp and screen? More profoundly seated in many minds may be a lurking notion that the excesses and failures of the great moral crusade stimulated in the public attitude toward law in general a glacial drift—from the cheerful irreverence which William Dean Howells once suggested as characteristic of Americans to a disrespect for authorities that makes for an uneasy alliance between the criminal class and the rest of us. The purposeful lawlessness of "demonstrators," the monolithic disregard for the rules that is symbiotic with one-issue political agitation, the sneaking suspicion of hypocrisy in high places—clerical as well as political—all these seem to intertwine amid the remembrance of things in a not too distant past when idealism stirred a nation to believe for a time that it could make the world safe for Democracy and its own citizens secure from Demon Rum.

---

*Professors M. A. Amerine and V. L. Singleton explain that the Alicante Bouschet was "most sought-after" in the eastern U. S. because it had a tough skin that made it ship well and enabled thrifty vintners to add sugar and water for a second pressing of juice (*Wine: An Introduction*, 2d ed. [Berkeley, Calif., 1977], p. 288).

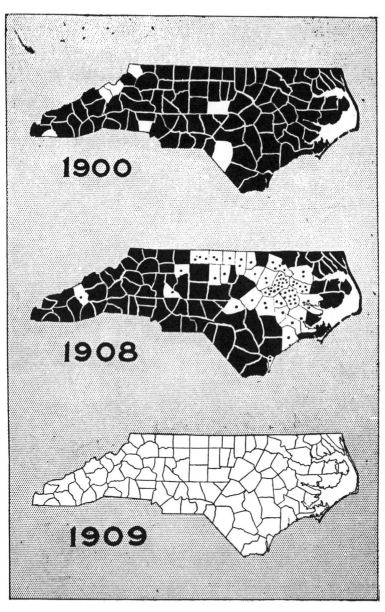

Wet and dry maps of North Carolina (*from* The Anti-Saloon
League Year Book, 1919)

Paul Garrett (*courtesy Mrs. L. J. Barden*)

CHAPTER V

Wine Concentrates and "Home Manufacture"

No American had a greater stake in the wine business at the time ethyl alcohol was made nationally disreputable by the Volstead Act than Paul Garrett. His scuppernong-flavored Virginia Dare was selling at the rate of a million cases a year, "the only wine whose name almost everybody knew," according to the editors of *Fortune*. Their survey of the prospects for "The Wines of America," published in February, 1934,[1] hailed him as "the number 1 advocate of making the U. S. a wine-drinking country." Beneath his picture, showing him looking more like a benevolent professor of philosophy than a practical business baron, the layout man wrote merely "Virginia Dare." Enough said. There were also cuts of his winery at Penn Yan on Keuka Lake and of his vineyard not far off at lovely Bluff Point, where he had built a show-place home. At the time a *Fortune* reporter interviewed him, Garrett had moved from the Finger Lakes region to an apartment on East Seventy-ninth Street in New York City. His business headquarters were in the Bush Terminal in Brooklyn where a huge blending and bottling establishment bore the name Garrett and Company.

In addition to plants in North Carolina and Penn Yan and Brooklyn, Garrett's empire included holdings also at Canandaigua and Hammondsport in New York and others in California, notably two thousand acres in San Bernardino County, where as early as 1911 he had established his Mission Vineyard and Winery at Cucamonga. In the neighborhood of this vineyard were the vast acres of the gigantic Italian Vineyard Company, redeemed from the sand hills and jack rabbits by the industry of old Secondo Guasti; and not far off were the fields of the Padre Vineyard Company, both of which *Fortune* ranked among the five largest of some 240 companies operating California wineries at the time of Repeal. Their port wine had been among California's best. They had prospered mightily by shipping fresh grapes eastward for the benefit of home and bootleg cellar operations until prices toppled as a result of overproduction. Garrett led the way to partial recuperation in the county by having his winemaker Marius Biane add to excess wines beef extract, pepsin, and a variety of other ingredients to form a concoction named Virginia Dare Tonic, legally salable as a medicament.[2] He also promoted a cola-grape drink and tried to make a flavoring extract. During the sorrows of the Prohibition era Garrett must often have thought of the inventor of Peruna, flute-playing Dr. Samuel B. Hartman, who had once offered him a job as salesman.[3] The Guastis and the Padre people, as did many others, also put out tonics.

Unfermented juice from New York grapes sold better by far than that made in California. An experiment with Virginia Dare minus alcohol netted dismal results. Even champagne could qualify for medical prescriptions as the authorities had been forced to decree. Sacramental wines of course yielded a small but steady income, in consideration perhaps of his long-standing generosity to the clergy,* aided possibly a fraction by his turning over to the Episcopal Church the beautiful chapel built at Bluff Point in 1930 to honor his dead. Closing the press-house at Aberdeen was only one of the measures taken in the interest of economy. Believing, almost as an article of faith, that light wines are a food, a health-giving stimulant to body and mind, Garrett was sure that national Prohibition could not last. Moreover, about 1925 there seemed to be a shifting of sentiment. In the election of 1926 and afterward, John Barleycorn was increasingly a boon companion of candidates in the big cities. The business community appeared to be reacting against the overkill of fanatics bent on hampering even the use of alcohol by industry.†

The intellectuals burst into guffaws when the mogul of the Anti-Saloon League opined that printing George Washington's recipe for making beer on February 22 would be contrary to the law.[4] And the *American Mercury* booed at the boobs of the Dry forces in every issue. Employers who helped the Dry forces with funds with the view of cultivating sobriety among their workers tightened their purse strings. Even John D. Rockefeller, Sr., stopped contributing to the Anti-Saloon League. The

---

*For many years Garrett & Co. donated Virginia Dare to the Episcopal clergy of Halifax County, N.C. (J. W. McGwigan to present writer, Jan. 14, 1980).

†In the chapters on alcohol, William Haynes (*The American Chemical Industry*, III and IV [New York, 1945; 1948]) explains why many producers of ethyl alcohol were slack in holding to the rules. Only three of the large manufacturers of alcohol had escaped charges of infractions by the end of Prohibition.

workers themselves clamored for beer by passing resolutions in the meetings of their unions. Legislation sporadically introduced here and there in both East and West suggested a growing element of moderates who believed that light wines and beer might provide a way to escape from uncontrolled speakeasies, corruption of police, and the lurid crimes of hoodlums in whose underworld vocabularies *ethyl* and *methyl* passed as perhaps merely names for twin girls.

Unlike the case of most of the wine men of the West Coast, owning and managing farms was a relatively minor portion of Paul Garrett's business, though the vineyards he owned at one time or the other in North Carolina, Virginia, New York, and California were not exactly negligible. As previously mentioned, up to the very advent of national Prohibition he had been urging others to plant more scuppernongs. A titan among the makers and merchants of the wines of America, he was of course well aware of technical advances in his field. One such was the improvement of food concentrates—the results of which are now familiar to everyone who adds water to a can of frozen orange juice in preparation of breakfast. A harmless concentrate of grape juice could be made and shipped wherewith a purchaser was easily provided with the most essential ingredient of wine simply by adding water. Tests in the courts had at times upheld what appeared to be specific sanction in the Volstead Act: "The penalties provided by this Act shall not apply to a person for manufacturing nonintoxicating cider and fruit juice exclusively for use in his home." Competition in making grape concentrates would in all likelihood bring about an overburdened market, something evident enough in the plight of the raisin growers and those who specialized in table grapes, so called. Accordingly, a marketing cooperative was indicated. Cooperatives of course were nothing new to California fruit growers—but Garrett had something much bigger in mind.

Cooperation was also smiled upon by the federal government in its pre-New Deal efforts to cope with the agricultural surpluses that, following the First World War, had prevented the farmer from sharing equitably in slicing the pie of affluence—attaining "parity." In 1929, within three months of Herbert Hoover's inauguration, an Agricultural Marketing Act authorized a Federal Farm Board to promote the sale of farm products through agricultural cooperatives and stabilizing corporations; and a $500-million revolving fund was set up to provide low-interest loans to the cooperating agencies. In the first seven years of national Prohibition the acreage in table grapes in California had nearly trebled, that in grapes for raisins doubled, and that in juice grapes almost doubled. A bumper harvest in 1928 spelled ruin. The farm value of the raisin crop in 1920 approximated $42 million on 177,000 tons; in 1928 the crop of 261,000 tons brought little more than $10 million. The decline in the prices of the other kinds of grapes was likewise considerable. In 1927 the year-old California Vineyardists' Association in desperation appealed to Washington for a "czar" to direct efforts to dispose of the surplus, and Herbert Hoover, then Secretary of Commerce, chose for the job Donald D. Conn, a former railroad traffic expert who had worked with lumber interests and was then serving as managing director of the Vineyardists' Association. Raisin grapes were pushed with much hullabaloo about the iron in their contents, and little packages of Sun Maids took their place on the shelves of candy stores. But the halfhearted tearing up of vines, "raisinade," jellies, etc. failed to solve all the problems. At that point Garrett appears to have stepped in.

In 1929 he encouraged the organization of a cooperative called Fruit Industries, Inc. (later *Inc.* became *Ltd.*), throwing into the pot not only his California establishment but also his four New York wineries—at Penn Yan, Canandaigua, Hammondsport, and Brooklyn. The Guastis with their "biggest vineyard in the world" joined in, as did also the whopper Vineyardists' Association, along with a number of smaller growers. Preferred stock was issued to member concerns, and they were pledged to seek loans. Donald Conn was appointed managing director and acted as front man, Secondo Guasti II became president, and Garrett, apparently the brains of Fruit Industries, was named chairman of the board. The Federal Farm Board, through its subsidiary Grape Control Board, promised financial aid and contracted with the new corporation to dispose of surplus grapes by turning them into concentrates or any other suitable products.[5] A contest was held to provide a name for the chief goods to be produced, and Vine-Glo was decided upon by the growers in preference to runner-up Merri-Cal.

Everywhere, except in Missouri, advertisements bloomed with the vigor of new hope, whole pages in certain big cities. "Now is the time," said the notices in the autumn of 1929, "to order your supply of VINE-GLO."

It can be made in your home in sixty days—a fine true-to-type guaranteed beverage ready for the Holiday Season.

VINE-GLO . . . comes to you in nine varieties, Port, Virginia Dare, Muscatel, Angelica, Tokay, Sauterne, Riesling, Claret and Burgundy. It is entirely legal in your home—but it must not be transported. . . .

You take absolutely no chance when you order your home supply of VINE-GLO which Section 29 of the National Prohibition Act permits you.[6]

The Big White Grape, under the name Paul Garrett had exploited it, was thus dignified by taking second place only to port in this list of honorable worthies. Before long stories were broadcast that prospects looked so good that Al Capone had offered to take over all of the new concentrate at a dollar a gallon. He was "righteously but wistfully" refused.[*]

There were no inconsiderable grounds for the assurances of "absolutely no chance" if one purchased a keg of Vine-Glo. In September, 1930, Amos Woodcock, newly appointed director of the U.S. Bureau of Prohibition, was quoted as pronouncing winemaking in private homes virtually beyond the reach of federal interference; the trade journal *Produce News* stated that there would be no "authorized" intervention; and the California Grape Control Board, representing varying interests, had emphatically announced: "Legal purchase and home consumption of juice grapes is assured."[7] When a reporter asked Alexander Legge, chairman of the Federal Farm Board, whether a part of the huge loan made to California growers was to be used to process surplus grapes for such home consumption he merely laughed. In due season three and a half million dollars helped to send Vine-Glo on its way to the cellars. When its general manager was forced to clear up the gossip about public funds supplied Fruit Industries, Conn explained that the cooperative had been organized only after conferences "with all interested departments of the Government."[8] In New York and elsewhere there were rumors that the arrest of a Vine-Glo seller had been hushed up, whereas salesmen dispensing a rival product called Vino Sano were prosecuted. The now celebrated instructions for the use of the rival Vino Sano, a mass of dried grapes shaped like a brick, read as follows:

Dissolve one brick in one gallon of plain water. Treat this exactly as you would freshly pressed fruit juices for home use.

Sugar may be added according to taste, usually one pound for the dry types [of wine], two pounds for the sweet types. The beverage should be consumed within five days, otherwise, and in summer temperature, it might ferment and become wine.[9]

---

[*]*Fortune* twice repeated the gossip (IV [1931], 56; and V [1932], 35).

Every knowledgeable person must have believed that the legal requirements affecting the operations of Fruit Industries had been carefully scrutinized by the corporation's chief counsel, none other than the very able former assistant attorney general of the United States. Under her jurisdiction had been tax laws and federal prisons as well as Prohibition, and she had only recently resigned and set up offices in Washington and Los Angeles. This attorney was Mabel Walker Willebrandt, appointed by President Harding in 1921 when she was but thirty-two years old. Clear-headed, hard-working, with no foibles save perhaps the habit of munching raw cabbage while reading in bed, Mrs. Willebrandt was a pioneer in advocating the legal rights of women, and during her term of office instituted the first federal rehabilitation center for female criminals. But her accomplishments—and her superb talents—have been obscured by her main governmental duties. In 1925 alone, more than 45,000 cases involving Prohibition had been tried under her direction. Admiring editorialists called her "the bootleggers' Nemesis." She was led to give up governmental work by the desire to spend more time with an adopted daughter and also by the handsome retainer proffered by the newly developing aircraft industry which hired her as Washington representative and interpreter of state and federal laws affecting their interests. Her friend, the grape growers' chief spokesman, Thomas C. Gregory of San Francisco, probably solicited her services for Garrett and his associates. Naturally, the howls and the jeers were many when the news leaked that she was acting as chief counsel for Fruit Industries. The satirist Ray T. Tucker characterized her emergence as "super-lawyer for the grape concentrate interests" as a transformation of "the Carrie Nation of the drys" into "the Clara Barton of the wets."[10] Al Smith, speaking to an enthusiastic audience of beer lovers in Newark, New Jersey, boomed out:

I congratulate the Fruit Industries in securing the services of so competent a person as Mabel. She did two things for them, two wonderful things. She convinced the Department of Justice that this 12 per cent wine was not intoxicating. That was some stunt when you figure that old Andy Volstead fixed it at half of one per cent, and she jumped it up 11–½ percent and still robbed it of its intoxicating character. But she did something else for them that was equally important. She got the Farm Board to lend them $20,000,000.[11]

Most remarkably, Fruit Industries initially secured the endorsement of the superintendent of the Anti-Saloon League of California, Arthur H. Briggs, D.D. He personally pacified the national policy-making groups of the Dry brethren by arguing that Vine-Glo was perfectly legal under federal law and explaining that the directors of its sponsoring firm were really prohibitionists at heart. The prefabricated winemaking in private homes, he observed, "must be watched critically but sympathetically." [12] One suspects that Chairman of the Board Paul Garrett must have had a long—and pleasant—chat with the Reverend Doctor Briggs.

Despite such worthy friends, the early prospects for Vine-Glo faded away when Judge Merrill E. Otis ruled on dispensers of grape concentrates in the U.S. District Court for the Western District of Missouri in the case of *U.S. v. Brunett et al.,* tried on October 16, 1931, in Kansas City. Ukiah Grape Products Company, a New Jersey corporation, and its Kansas City sales manager were indicted for violations of the Volstead Act, "against the peace and dignity of the United States of America," their offense having taken place about a year earlier. By mutual consent a jury trial was waived. It was evident that grape syrup (probably of the brand called Caligrapo) was shipped from California to New York and there held in the defendant company's factory until orders were received. Then the requisite syrup was mixed with water, sugar, and flavoring matter, put in casks or kegs, shipped by rail to a district office nearest the purchaser, and turned over to him with instructions on further procedures. When delivered, the juice retailed at three to five dollars per gallon, of which the salesman received twenty-five percent. Sales Manager Albert Brunett's memorandum book, seized in the raid on the company's offices, revealed a full set of instructions for his agents, including a few sample "approaches" to prospective customers, who were to be sought only from among the ranks of business and professional people. Here is one of them: "My name is so-and-so. Some people around here call me King Bootlegger because I have called on numerous friends of yours, and you have been recommended to me by so-and-so. . . ." Even the arrangements for the office were carefully planned, it was obvious, for the office girl, so the memorandum book read, "must be pretty, but not fat, of good family, a Protestant and a prohibitionist." [13]

Judge Otis, however, provided little *divertissement* in writing his opinion. Point by point, with the ideal symmetry of Aristotle's Square, he demolished the arguments of Ukiah's lawyers and demonstrated that "one who contributes some essential service to the creation of wine is engaged in the manufacture of wine." The Eighteenth Amendment "may not be wise," he admitted, but it is the law. Ironically, he observed of the chief defendant: "A corporation which boasts that its assets are of the value of a million dollars and that its business is nation wide [*sic*] claims the protection of the cloak which Congress designed for the housewife and the home owner who make non-intoxicating fruit juices for their families."[14] The case was never appealed though frequently cited. Judge Otis well deserved the Phi Beta Kappa key dangling from his watch chain.

Mrs. Willebrandt lost no time in advising: "Stop making the Vine-Glo"—and the glow faded. Most of the thousands of gallons on hand eventually went the way of discarded vintages, into the brandy stills. Under the name Vintners, however, some of it was reportedly sold in New York City in 1933 through the medium of the erstwhile high-class importers Alex D. Shaw & Company. They obtained the concentrate, so it was said, from Vineyardists, Inc., of Penn Yan, and the purchasers included some of the tony Fifth Avenue set.[15] Of course there were howls. Mrs. Willebrandt and officials of the Prohibition Bureau were charged with deception, and President Hoover himself was held responsible because he had sanctioned the schemes for disposing of the surpluses in grapes when he was Secretary of Commerce.[16]* Dr. Briggs promptly ate crow, and in his propaganda organ, the *California Liberator*, commented: "Fruit Industries is charging the Federal Government with bad faith. That is the way the sinner usually feels about it in a situation like this."[17] He did not say how he felt.

With its widely heralded concentrate eliminated, the mammoth cooperative began to crumble. The "little fellows" who dropped out complained that they had been tricked. Garrett withdrew his empire in August, 1933. In 1934 *Fortune* stated that Fruit Industries then represented only about thirty percent of California's wine production but was still the largest business of the sort in the nation. In the later years of national Prohibition it had been assumed that the company accounted for more than half of all the wine made commercially. The Italian Vineyards of the Guastis waited until 1940 to pull out, and ten years later Fruit Industries assumed the name of its chief remaining constituent, the California Wine Association. Ultimately, the last eleven members of the Association trickled down in 1971 to just one.[18]

When Garrett withdrew he found that the only way he could recover the right to use the name Virginia Dare was to forfeit the immense stores of wine held in his California plants. He did not hesitate to sacrifice the

---

*Conn undoubtedly had discussed the matter with Hoover but carefully refrained from claiming that concentrates had been mentioned.

several million dollars entailed.* The name Virginia Dare, "perhaps the most valuable in the whole industry,"[19] would—and did—recoup the loss.

---

*Fruit Industries continued to hold the rights to Virginia Dare Tonic as long as any was left.

CHAPTER VI

Post-Repeal

The thirteen years of national Prohibition scarcely served as a pause that refreshed the wine industry of the United States. In 1933 California tripled its average production for the years just prior to the onset of the great experiment with pretty poor stuff. Its best wine grapes had given way to "good shippers"; many of its chief growers were erstwhile fruit dealers to whom the aroma of a jug of vin ordinaire was bouquet delicate enough; various distinguished wineries like that of Krug, "the wine king of the Napa Valley," were closed, sometimes their cooperage destroyed; trained help was scarce or nonexistent; and distribution often rested in the hands of converted bootleggers. Most of the early post-Repeal offerings to Bacchus, ill made and insufficiently aged, were downright unpalatable. To restore standards, a few of the old-line firms sought state or federal regulation by founding the Wine Institute, which also encouraged the repeal or revision of such laws of the several states as militated against the importation or sale of their wares. The chaotic local legislation resembled a maze of brambles and thickets through which the industry was forced to run after Uncle Sam took down the barbed wire. Quite as important was the impetus given by the institute to advertising and to the promotion of sales, endeavors in which Californians have not been negligent.[1]

New York vintners fared somewhat better in several ways, though skilled help for the making of their highly reputed sparkling wines had to be reassembled or newly trained, and tax laws of course were as burdensome to them as to the Californians who outproduced them eight or ten to one. A fair number of the Finger Lakes' houses of chief renown remained in business, for example the Pleasant Valley Wine Company, noted for its Great Western Champagne. Its later owner, the Taylor firm, likewise survived, though it possessed just four buildings in the late 1930s. Another was the Urbana Wine Company, dating from 1865, which had supplied Paul Garrett with bulk wines when he ran short of scuppernongs in his early days in Halifax County.[2] The New York growers had nothing quite like the Wine Institute to voice their needs, but one of their number appeared as a spokesman of proved capacity and long experience. His own people, the southerners, called him "The Boss"; Californians and associates of Fruit Industries gave him the title "Captain"; but soon everyone was following the example of the magazine *Fortune*, which in its survey of the prospects for wines in February, 1934, dubbed him "Dean" of American winemen. In addition to length of service dating back to 1876 in which he had dealt with every phase of the business, from planting the vines to advertising the end product, he had literally spanned the country with his press-houses, seventeen of them by 1919—in North Carolina, Virginia, New York, Ohio, Missouri, and California.[3] Adding to his position as spokesman for the whole industry was his new location in New York City, business capital and eccentric ganglion of the information media and commercial ballyhoo. His opinions were expressed not only in interviews but also in three pamphlets published in 1934 and 1935 and in a letter to the *New York Times* dated December 5, 1935, later described in that paper's obituary of him as "a Bacchic prose pastoral of the American Grape."[4]

Much of what the Dean had to say was a repetition of what he had been harping on of old and put into print in his elegant brochure of 1905: wine is a food and should be treated as such taxwise; the "fetish" of the superiority of foreign wines is to be deplored; nobody can prove we are a nation of hard-liquor drinkers until we give "the wholesome, health-giving" beverage a chance; the example of France and Italy proves that the use of wine as part of a daily diet would "forever remove the vexatious problem of intemperance." This last argument, almost as hoary as the temperance movement itself, had been brushed off and newly put back into service in the persistent efforts to revamp the Volstead Act and, conjoined with similar grounds for the clamor for beer, had brought on the slogan "Light Wines and Beer" as a pry against the weight of Prohibition. In North Carolina and elsewhere exemption of light wines and beer was one of the aims of the earliest pieces of legislation designed to modify the restrictive liquor code, though rarely did the enabling bills survive the opposition of the Drys. In time, of course, the panacea of light wines and beer was to fade away, as did also the belief that since bathtub gin had been so widely adopted as the tipple sought from bootleggers, the post-Repeal era would see whiskey playing second fiddle. What Doctor Samuel Johnson said about the freedom of the will applied also in this connection: all argument was for it; all experience against.

Garrett's arguments, however, were persuasive. In 1918, he pointed out, the year prior to national Prohibition, 51,000,000 gallons of wine were produced domestically in the nation and three million were imported. Ten years later, of an estimated 150,000,000 gallons consumed, only a few thousand had been manufactured abroad and only five million produced legally, for sacramental and medical purposes. Since the foreign-born population had not increased notably, following the immigration controls instituted in 1918, the evidence pointed to a fabulous growth in the popularity of wines. Suppose the trend continued during the decade following Repeal? Even when one reduced the figures by two-thirds and assumed that Americans would buy twelve gallons per year each—rounded out to about a bottle a week, with a few over for birthdays and Christmas—the demand would be ten times more than the country had ever produced, and five million people would be employed in the process. "The opportunity has never existed at any time in this or any other country," he urged, "millions of people are out of work and government agencies are trying to find work for them." Much of the land hitherto unproductive or withdrawn from agriculture in the effort to curb surpluses could grow wine grapes. Federal and state funds should be put into the service of growers, for no investment would be more likely to be self-liquidating—provided, of course, that shackling regulations, restrictions, and crippling taxes were eased. "There is more substantial argument for the development of viticulture than for the development of the cigarette habit or even of the automobile habit," he concluded in *Wine as an American Industry*.[5] On the front page of his pamphlet appear these words: "How an encouraged and expanded American Wine Industry can accomplish re-employment of millions, a new money crop for the farmer, true temperance for the nation."

The old Dean apparently was quite as aware of what would appeal to the times as he had been at the turn of the century. And he was equally concerned with advertising the Big White Grape. On the back of the pamphlet he put the picture of the old scuppernong vine from Tyrrell County with an explanatory note and in another publication devoted to *Viticulture in the United States* he reproduced the same cut along with these words: "This grand old Scuppernong Vine, discovered in 1585 and still alive after 350 years' vicissitudes, supplied in 1835 many of the roots of the Medoc vineyards. It is located in Tyrrell County, North Carolina, not far from Roanoke Island, the scene of Raleigh's 'Lost Colony.' It might be appropriately called the Mother of the American Wine Industry."[6] As principal owner of the Medoc Vineyards he could lay claim to possessing a connection with the first child of English parentage born on American soil as well as with the grape whose product he had named in her honor.

More historically sound, however, were Garrett's reminders that the South had missed a golden opportunity when the "prohibition sentiment" put an end to the dream of its finding a Bacchic bonanza. A considerable part of his essay on American viticulture, however, is devoted to demonstrating that a new era was at hand, the White House, for example, having proclaimed that none but native vintages were to be served at dinners there,* and the time was ripe for planting the muscadines. "It may well be said," he averred, "that a Scuppernong vineyard of 25 or more acres is a literary man's Utopia and a lazy man's Paradise." More specifically, he claimed that, once established, the vines needed little labor beyond extending the supporting arbors and, what with a few pigs to keep the weeds down, expenses should not exceed five or ten dollars an acre. Basing his figures on an average yield of two to five tons of grapes, he estimated profits running from $75 to $100 per acre. He further cheered on prospective vineyardists by noting that "under the able direction of the Federal Relief Administration, a beginning has been made by planting thousands of acres in North Carolina, South Carolina, and Georgia."[7]

The pertinency and potency of Garrett's appeal to the South can scarcely be imagined today. The Sun Belt, as we call it now, bears little resemblance to the South described by Franklin D. Roosevelt in 1938 as "the nation's number one economic problem." Even before his inauguration on March 4, 1933, the president and his advisers had been at work on farm legislation with a view to scrapping the Federal Farm Board, consolidating all agricultural credit agencies, and creating an allotment plan.[8] The situation was indeed grave. Surplus production with declining prices for agricultural products, combined with the greatest economic depression in American history, had run up foreclosures on farm mortgages to the rate of 20,000 a month in 1932, a year which saw a fourth of the state of Mississippi forced into sale. A South Dakota wife pitifully wrote to her local paper: "My husband had to buy a pair of shoes. To pay

---

*Garrett gallantly attributed the decision to Mrs. Roosevelt. The *New York Times*, Dec. 2, 1934, noted the announcement (p. 14).

the price [$4] we brought to town twenty pounds of butter and twelve dozen eggs. That just paid for the shoes."[9] In 1935 two out of three farm operators in the South were tenants—more than two-thirds of them blacks. Nearly a fourth of these whites and more than half of the blacks[10] were sharecroppers. What happened when acreage in cotton or corn or tobacco was reduced with the purpose of eliminating surplus crops? The abject plight of the tenants—one in about every four southerners—, long inured as they were to the poverty implicit in ignorance, made the Snopeses of Faulkner's tales, the grotesques of Erskine Caldwell's fictions, or the Okies of John Steinbeck's *Grapes of Wrath* seem like realism without the *sur*.

Getting some of these innocents onto small plots of land and showing them how to make a living by raising scuppernongs might well seem to be more tangible than grasping at straws, particularly when the dean of American vintners gave assurance that he would buy every grape offered for sale. The prospect apparently seemed worthier than the measure proposed by an Illinois congressman, to require all gasoline used in automobiles to contain ten percent of alcohol made from agricultural products.* At least the Federal Emergency Relief Administration gave the scuppernongs a try. "A new money crop for the farmer." "Re-employment of millions." Maybe not millions, but still—.

Among the many relief agencies that mushroomed during the Great Depression, the FERA dispensed funds through a bewildering conglomeration of subsidiaries; among them was the North Carolina Relief Administration. Projects drawing funds under its auspices were required to be "socially and economically desirable" as well as needed. Moreover, at first they were intended to be self-liquidating within a reasonable length of time. One of the activities proposed was the establishment in Eastern Carolina of twenty-five units, of 200 tenant families each, on tracts of land purchased with federal funds, to be farmed for the first three years on a community basis. Chickens, cows, pigs, and mules would be supplied. The first objective was to provide food for the inhabitants, but such other crops would be raised as might be determined by the Secretary of Agriculture or some other satisfactory authority.[11] It was just one of the means of helping the estimated 10,000 families east of Raleigh, mainly tenants or jobless refugees from cities, who in 1935 "had no ar-

---

*His bill, revised, never emerged from committee, for it was believed that it would run up the price of auto fuel and encourage even more planting of corn (William Haynes, *American Chemical Industry* [New York, 1954], V, 140–41).

rangements with any landlord to make a crop and who had no other employment sufficient to enable them to earn a subsistence." Three-fifths were Negroes.

As previously recorded in chapter 3, long before the coming of national Prohibition Paul Garrett had been persistently urging farmers to plant more scuppernongs and, to meet the demands for his Virginia Dare, had agreed to buy the harvests at prices insuring a profit. Long before the advent of national Prohibition a Moore County nurseryman, like some others, had pointed out the quick and easy path to prosperity beckoned by the *Vitis rotundifolia*, there had been a cooperative vineyard of sorts planned in Gates County, and not far off an effort had been made to attract New England workmen to settle on small tracts in Hyde County to make an easy living by raising the delicious muscadines. But someone must have sold the idea anew to the central authorities in Washington in charge of agricultural relief, for the growing of grapes to supplement the income of rehabilitated families was planned for appropriate areas in several of the southern states, from Louisiana on up into Virginia. Two million vines were envisaged.

In 1935 a brochure put out by the North Carolina Emergency Relief Administration, under the aegis of Mrs. Thomas O'Berry, described initial steps as follows:

North Carolina is the original habitat of the scuppernong grape. The counties of the Upper Coastal Plain are well adapted to its culture and in these counties there are many home vineyards. In several of these counties there are commercial vineyards most of which have been allowed to deteriorate during the last several years. It is believed that it is possible to revive the grape industry and to expand it within this and other southern states. This will give a considerable section a new non-competitive industry which can be used to supplement the income of rehabilitation families.

Under advice of Dr. F. G. Woodruff [*sic*], vines leased from individual growers are now being layered, with a view to producing rooted cuttings for distribution to relief clients, and to other southern states which do not have sufficient vines to meet their needs.* Forty-six thousand four hundred thirty-three vines have already been cut and sold to Georgia, Arkansas, Florida and Louisiana. The income from vines already sold is in excess of the cost of propagation. In addition to shoots transported to these states, vines will be transplanted to the farms of R. R. clients in sections where small vineyards will be profitable as a means of cash income. [12]

*J. G. Woodroof, a Georgia scientist in charge, described the difficulties in rooting the cuttings, made from "five strains of Scuppernongs," plus the Hunt, Thomas, James, and the male pollinators used (*Proceedings of the American Society for Horticultural Science*, XXXIII [1935], 447–49).

The Carolina vinegrowing was carried on in Beaufort, Bladen, Columbus, Cumberland, Duplin, Hoke, Moore, Richmond, Robeson, Sampson, and Scotland counties. And it apparently was the first of the state relief projects to amortize its costs—another triumph for the Big White Grape and its cousins.

Further evidence of the extent of the planned grape production appeared in *Rural Rehabilitation* for February 15, 1935, a sheet issued by the FERA.[13] There it was reported that several southeastern Louisiana counties were in process of planting 20,000 of the vines from North Carolina, and 1500 more were destined for two REA communities in Georgia. "Next year," it was promised, "a million vines will be available from propagation projects of the relief administration in North Carolina." The article also announced that a contract had been made with a winemaker to pay thirty-five dollars per ton for the grapes to come three years later, and furthermore, he would erect a processing plant to take care of the output.

Almost certainly Paul Garrett was the man who thus collaborated with the venture in rural relief. His activities in behalf of the huge combine Fruit Industries had involved a close relationship with bureaucrats of the Department of Agriculture, and he could offer assurance that the scuppernongs would not further glut the already overburdened grape market, a matter of concern to the well-organized and politically efficient California growers. Moreover, no vintner in the nation could more credibly offer to buy the harvest. As has been evident, long before the Volstead Act had been drafted by Wayne B. Wheeler, Garrett and Company had run short of the muscadines, and now that he was carried away in his belief that light wines were going to boom he had good reason for contemplating a really enormous "expanding spree." He erected a new plant in Atlanta to make concentrate from the supplies of grapes anticipated from the southeastern districts, remodeled the warehouse at Aberdeen, put up receiving tanks alongside the railroad tracks at Enfield to take care of the juice pressed in Halifax County, and refurbished the equipment in Wilmington obtained from the Bear family. At Aberdeen he processed grapes and berries received from the Carolinas and Virginia but shipped the resultant wine for finishing and bottling to headquarters in Brooklyn. Likewise, from Wilmington scuppernong concentrate made its way thither in 8000-gallon tank cars.*

---

*Information from Robert L. Walker, one of his chief associates. The *Raleigh News and Observer*, Aug. 24, 1935, carried a story on plans for improving the Aberdeen plant.

To round up whatever grapes and berries might be already available, Garrett ranged through the southern states, energizing production with promises to purchase the crops. After contracting for dewberries in eastern Carolina he appeared on Roanoke Island in August, 1937, where he signed an agreement with Guy H. Lennon for the entire output of the now fabled Old Mother Vineyard. A reporter who interviewed him the same day quoted him as declaring that the eastern section of the state was overlooking a vastly important industry by neglecting its famous grapes and that if 200 to 300 acres of them could be contracted for he would establish a plant at Manteo. At the time, he complained, he had to go as far as California for seventy-five percent of the grapes needed for his business.[14] Both abroad and at home he continued to bubble with the hope that wine would help solve the unemployment problem, and in December, 1935, in a letter to the *New York Times* he went so far as to state that not only "millions of workers" but "perhaps all of our unemployed" might find jobs if adult Americans would take to the use of light wines.

In his interviews and pamphlets Garrett inevitably put in a few good words for his own firm, usually mentioning its presumed antiquity of about a century, dating from 1835, when Sidney Weller had started farming in Halifax County and prepared the way for the business eventually obtained by his uncle and directed now by himself. Always he exalted the scuppernong and continued to reproduce a picture of the old vine from Tyrrell County. But he did not neglect to put up placards and posters in stores and dispensaries, and he took to the radio by means of a singing commercial with the refrain "Say it again——Virginia Dare." He was the first wine man in the country, it is believed, to indulge in such modernity.[15] His *Notes on Wine and Its Service* was illustrated with pictures in color as well as the wonted black and white cut of himself, studious in pose and pen in hand. This folder contained a brief homily on wine as food, a few explanations of the chief kinds of wines and the sorts befitting various occasions and ended with a list of his own vintages. Names like Minnehaha and Hiawatha were now discarded, and instead he labeled his wares more simply. First, naturally enough, was Virginia Dare, "the incomparable dessert and all service wine . . . favorite of the American hostess"—sweet in taste and available as white or red. Then there was its dry counterpart named Paul Garrett, also to be had in red or white; and finally came the sparkling, the famous Paul Garrett Special and Paul Garrett Brut. Of course he sold also blackberry and the conventional port, sherry, etc.

How much scuppernong resided in the bottles no one can say. Leon Adams remembered the Virginia Dare he sampled in the 1930s as "bland-tasting California wine." Garrett probably varied the contents in accordance with supplies available at a given time but depended on the muscadines for bouquet and fruity flavor. He boasted that his wines were American—"not imitations" of foreign varieties and had "more taste" than most of the California "imported" sorts. He noted, however, that his vineyards were located in that state as well as in the Finger Lakes section of New York and in North Carolina, "where we grow the full flavored grape called the Scuppernong."*

When national Prohibition ended, Paul Garrett was the only man in the country ready to do business in every state that allowed wines to be sold. And he profited mightily by the fact. So did the Big White Grape. But the grandiose scheme of newly rehabilitated sharecroppers making a cash crop by raising grapes was quickly suppressed. The farm bloc during the days of the New Deal was captained by southerners, but the senators and congressmen from the Sahara of the Bozart, as Mencken called the South, owed overriding allegiance to Dry forces as well as deference to economic pressures, and Rexford Tugwell or Harry Hopkins or whoever it was who originally sanctioned the project on high lapsed into quiescence. The government spending money to make liquor? It was too much like the Devil quoting Scripture or maybe even like celebrating a black mass in front of a Methodist altar. Some of the grapes that got planted, however, survived the storm—and when the Farm Security Administration took over the task of relocating displaced tenants, a project started near Creswell was named Scuppernong Farms, appropriately enough, for in the near neighborhood the Pettigrews had made some of the first wine ever given the name of the Big White Grape.[16]

Notes on Wine and Its Source also indicates that he was trying to retrieve vineyards in Virginia he had once apparently owned. Probably he encouraged the organization in 1934 of the Monticello Grape Growers Cooperative Association, led in Charlottesville by Bernard P. Chamberlain (information from Professor G. D. Oberle).

CHAPTER VII

Recent Effervescence

In 1923, with the Dry forces triumphant yet fearful of siren voices, North Carolina, like Ulysses, bound itself to the mast by means of the bone-dry Turlington Act; a decade later it voted by more than two to one against repealing Prohibition. Nevertheless, within a few years thereafter, surprisingly and inconsistently, its legislature sanctioned local option by counties, under the regulation of Alcoholic Beverage Control Boards. Most of the eastern section of the state promptly voted wet. Beer and light wines, not unnaturally, were the forerunners of ardent spirits, and on May 10, 1935, an act was ratified which not only permitted the manufacture of light wines but also delegated to the State Department of Agriculture the duty of instructing citizens in grape growing and viniculture. Sales rights were granted to food stores.[1] In 1941, within the ABC counties fortified wines were allowed to be sold in hotels and restaurants as well as in grocery stores. The coincidence of the legislation of 1935 with the attempt to plant scuppernongs as an aid to rural relief and with Paul Garrett's energetic efforts to insure supplies for his Virginia Dare may not have been wholly fortuitous.

Response to the opportunity for producing wine was, however, languid. Out-of-state wineries remained the chief outlets for North Carolina grapes. Small country vintners were sometimes scared out of business when the counties in which they were located either went dry or teetered on the verge of doing so. The Census of 1940 reported only two licensed commercial wineries in the state, the same number recorded for Georgia, Florida, and Louisiana each. Arkansas was then Dixie's wineland with eight. The southern states in general were still regarded as the "Bible Belt" that the scoffer Henry Mencken had derided two decades earlier. The nation at large, however, also failed to sustain the vision of a triumph for beer and Bacchus prophesied just before Repeal. Whiskey was still king; low consumer income blighting the days of the Great Depression scarcely harmonized with wining and dining. California's huge crop of grapes harvested in 1937 was greeted not so much by rejoicing in harvest festivals as by appeals of growers to the Federal Commodity Credit Corporation for help. Crop reduction, conversion of grapes into alcohol, and other desperate measures were prompted by continuing distress in the industry.[2] Eastern grape growers fared somewhat better as the demand for their wines actually increased for a time; but in North Carolina the total number of grapevines registered by the Census Bureau declined from 555,624 in 1935 to 529,185 in 1940.

Despite his constant encouragement of southern growers to plant more grapes and berries, Paul Garrett apparently was never able to restore to his blended wines their original constituency. Carloads of wines or juice or concentrate rolled from California and New York into the Bush Terminal in Brooklyn to provide the main ingredient, though not the special flavor and aroma, of his continuingly popular Virginia Dare, red and white. As the years passed he was probably too busy to be worried about the failure of his predictions that wine production would help mightily in ending the plight of the jobless. Things changed for the better. Forlorn veterans of World War I selling apples on street corners faded further from memory as the Great Depression terminated in a boom of industries activated by a new war. Even cheerless houses along the roadsides in North Carolina, disconsolate symbols of hard times, here and there began to gleam with fresh paint. And on March 20, 1940, Paul Garrett died at the age of seventy-six. He had gone to work up to three days before he was stricken. The *New York Times* in its obituary made up a shortage of information by levying on his letter to that paper containing praise of native American grapes and a tribute to a great vine in Tyrrell County.[3] That was appropriate, surely, for, next to the United States Department of Agriculture, Garrett was the greatest benefactor of the scuppernong.

As everyone knows, a revolution in the American wine industry has taken place since the dean of American vintners passed from the scene. The plant breeders have worked miracles in developing desired characteristics in new varieties of grapes; the science of viticulture, aided by state and federal funds, has become almost an art, though that term is perhaps more aptly applied to the companion science of enology. Stemming from headquarters such as the University of California at Davis and several other centers, the techniques of winemaking have been advanced to the point that the corpus of knowledge dealing with wine chemistry alone is enough to warrant a separate academic discipline. A visitor to a large modern winery stands amazed at the now conventional mammoth steel tanks controlled by thermostats. It seems unbelievable that as recently as 1904 at the St. Louis Exposition people marvelled at the "greatest wine vat in the world," erected by coopers imported from France and holding all of 14,300 gallons.*

Radical changes in ownership are likewise indicative of a revolution in the American wine industry; they help to explain not the least part of the vastly increased consumption of its products. Premonitory of what was to come a couple of decades later was the entrance into the business during World War II of large whiskey firms. With the manufacture of beverage alcohol thwarted by war restrictions and even with hopes of export markets resultant from the overrunning of France by the Germans, firms like Schenley, National Distillers, Hiram Walker, and Seagram noted the straws in the wind and cast covetous eyes on vineyards. When independent wine bottlers and dealers complained of shortages in 1943 and growers began to show fright in California, a state then estimated as producing 85 percent of the nation's wines, the Department of Justice began an investigation. The following year, the Washington representative of the Wine Institute, Edward W. Wootton, testified before a group of concerned Senators that distillers had gained control of more than 25 percent of the wine inventories and crushed 19 percent of California's grapes.[4] Statistics apparently continued to look good—even better—to investors, the *New York Times*, for example, reporting in 1949 an increase of commercially produced wines in the nation from 68 million gallons to about 126 within a decade. Monthly consumption was estimated at 10 million gallons, with California supplying 87.8 percent, the other states 9.7 percent, and imports making up the remainder.[5] When, however, there followed a lull in the boom and some proclaimed the excitement a kind of false dawn, several of these new owners sold out, only to reenter the business later. National Distillers, for example, after having disposed of three wineries in California, revived interest to the point of acquiring the prestigious Almaden Vineyard. Toward the end of the 1960s, as the wine boom showed many signs of becoming somewhat of a craze, big business expanded its hold. A consortium of older California wineries called United Vintners became a wholly owned subsidiary of Heublein, noted for a brand of vodka named Smirnoff and much else besides, including of late Kentucky Fried Chicken. Its wholesale invasion of the wine business

---

*Dimensions: 17½ feet long and the same in diameter. The wood came from Mississippi, Kentucky, and Tennessee (J. W. Hanson, *The Official History of the Fair St. Louis 1904* [St. Louis, Mo., 1904], p. 228).

in 1972 prompted a complaint from the Federal Trade Commission which led to a court decision that the company should divest itself of United Vintners, an order quickly appealed. Names like Italian Swiss Colony, Inglenook, Petri, and Beaulieu were gathered in its daisy chain as Heublein continued to expand.*

Rosy prospects continued to lure investors as the 1960s gave way to the next decade. In September, 1973, the authoritative Bank of America in reporting on the wine industry raised its prediction for 1980 to 650 million gallons and estimated prospective per capita consumption for the nation as 2.9 gallons, compared with 1.6 in 1972. Such optimism seemed justified when the figures showed wine distribution in the United States as having risen 65 percent during the five-year period prior to the report. The bank listed various reasons in explaining the phenomenon: rising income as well as growth in the older population, better products, more effort to promote them, and fewer burdens in the way of legal restrictions. Notice was also taken of the lowering of the drinking age in several states, a shift in public taste away from sweet fortified wines to light table varieties, the vogue of "pop" wines made from apples and other fruits, and the stimulus to sale provided by restaurants and grocery stores.†

A few months prior to the Bank of America report the *Wall Street Journal*, commenting on recent activities among investors in the wine business, mentioned Beatrice Foods as having taken the plunge, Trans World Airlines as looking into similar prospects, the Northeast Industries as having formed a new company to import French vintages. Among the firms already diversifying into wine were Coca-Cola Bottling of New York, which had acquired the Mogen David Wine Company in 1970 and later added Tribuno Vermouth to its holdings. Nestlé, with its wine business under the name Crosse and Blackwell Vintage Cellars, was also noted.[6] When the Federal Trade Commission in 1974 challenged (in vain) the acquisition of Franzia Brothers by the Coca-Cola Bottling Company of New York, its lawyers presumably did not know that the parent Coca-Cola corporation was on the prowl that in 1977 resulted in a merger

---

*Standard and Poor's records in outline the mergers of many of the largest firms, as does also Adams in *Wines of America*. As wine became more newsworthy newspapers like the *New York Times* and the *Wall Street Journal* carried such information regularly.

†The bank stated that California produced 71 percent of the wines sold in 1972, the other states 15 percent, while imports made up the rest. The proportion, but not the quantity, coming from California was expected to decline. France and Italy were still far ahead in per capita consumption: 28.3 gallons in 1971 for the former; 29.3 for the latter (*New York Times*, Sept. 22, 1973, p. 16).

with the huge Taylor Wine Company and thereafter was to add materially to a veritable vinous empire. Gossip had it that the soft-drink moguls had first made a try for the firm the Gallo Brothers had built so successfully after starting up in 1933. Even the Getty Oil people undertook a wine business near Fresno, California.

These shifts in ownership are merely illustrative of a larger trend. The scurrying in banks and boardrooms involved in these transactions was accompanied by, even at times inspired by, other manifestations of wine fervor. (Or is it a remittent fever endemic since the earliest days of colonial settlement?) The "little fellows" also ventured back into the wine business, sometimes merely as a hobby, and by the dawn of the 1980s "Mom and Pop" establishments were scattered in appropriate spots all over the country. Wine books at times picked up surprising sales. The publishers of one entitled *The Art of Making Wine* claimed a sale of a hundred thousand copies in little more than a couple of months and guessed that twice that number of Americans were then indulging in the art in their own cellars or kitchens.[7] An enterprising outfit, California-based naturally, offered for sale to the novice a "wine-tape" designed to aid in the proper pronunciation of the names of the several wines; price $12.50. Junkets to vineyard regions of Europe, already initiated by the American Express Company in the 1950s, waxed in popularity, as did tours of domestic Bacchic shrines. In the highly favored Napa Valley traffic congestions put a severe burden on thirsty pilgrims as well as on the budgets of those who offered wine tasting as a bid for future sales. The ramification of the heightened fervor is suggested by such novel phenomena as the employment of wine stewards in certain supermarkets, the serving of wines on domestic air flights, the multiplication of wine and cheese parties or a vogue for imbibing a glass of chablis instead of a martini at cocktail lounges and even at business lunches. Fabulous prices reportedly paid for old vintages at auctions became standard items in newspapers. Studies of the medicinal virtues of wines were revived, and of course importers made efforts to share in the bonanza, a point well illustrated by the rash of Italian labels seen on the shelves of grocery stores. The novel Italianate "Always Elvis" brand, however, failed notably to replace Soave. Even as the statistics for 1977 showed a 3 percent drop in the consumption of whiskey, an increase of 4 percent for beer but a jump of 12 percent for wine, the Treasury Department's alcohol division saw fit to urge stricter supervision of the labels on the bottles so that consumers might know better just what they might be purchasing.

Do such symptoms as recorded above really prove that Paul Garrett was only about one generation too early in prophesying a fundamental change in American drinking habits? Or do they merely reflect a quirk in fashions like the grape craze Americans spoke of in the late 1850s? For the nine months ending in June, 1979, total revenues from alcoholic beverages declined somewhat, but again those derived from the sale of beer and wine were up. One will have to postpone an answer to the question until more swallows have satisfied more summer thirsts. At all events, a historian may reasonably conclude that the "big interests" have demonstrated the effects of their mighty powers of promotion. At no time, anywhere, have so many millions of people been subjected to so much clever—and also foolish—advertising of wines. If the wine could remember it would never recall anything similar since the days when Anacreon sang its praises and Horace made "Old Falernian" a subject for poetry.

We turn now to the repercussions of the national wine boom in North Carolina and the effects of the recent effervescence on the muscadine. The frequent changes in ownership marking the history of the American wine industry since the days of the Great Drought are mirrored in the annals of the single vintage named Virginia Dare, which, it will be recalled, had carried the scuppernong flavor to national fame. As we have seen, Paul Garrett recovered his rights to the trade name when in 1933 he sundered connections with the great marketing cooperative Fruit Industries, and in exchange forfeited his California wine reserves worth many millions of dollars. The expensive gamble apparently paid off by the time of his death in 1940; at least his heirs resolved to continue the old Garrett and Company policy of expanding operations to keep ahead of demand. In 1943 they purchased a sizeable vineyard and winery at Ukiah, California, and two years later acquired control of the immense holdings of the historic Italian Vineyard Company at Guasti. Added to properties previously owned at Cucamonga, this gigantic tract made the firm the possessor of some 7,000 acres of grapes and of three of the largest processing plants on the West Coast. All of the final bottling, however, was concentrated at the warehouse at Guasti or at headquarters in the Bush Terminal in Brooklyn, until in 1958 the latter was closed and Virginia Dare, so it was said, became "a girl of the Golden West."[8] The size of the holdings in San Bernardino County in 1952 may be glimpsed through a local newspaper story which estimated the vineyard at Guasti as so large that if one single tractor did the plowing performed by the thirteen machines then employed there, it would have to travel a distance equal to a round trip between California and Chicago in order to cultivate the three million vines just once.[9]

When skyrocketing values of real estate in the Los Angeles area outdistanced profits derived from winemaking, Garrett and Company began to sell off some of its land, and in 1961 determined to liquidate its business altogether, so as to capitalize on the appreciated value of its assets. A Fresno firm, Alta Vineyards, quickly secured the rights to the Garrett labels, and when Alta merged with the Guild federation, centered at Lodi, the name Virginia Dare joined the wide assortment of brands controlled by the latter. The wine so denominated was far different from the various blends Paul Garrett had bottled. In 1966, under a franchise from Guild Wineries and Distilleries, a new firm in the Finger Lakes region, then called Canandaigua Industries, took over the name Virginia Dare and applied it to a whole line of table beverages most of them presumably made half and half from California and New York grapes. But Canandaigua's original owners, M. E. Sands and his son Marvin, chose to feature a rosé made of *labruscas* which they named Richards Wild Irish Rose. This was far and away their best-known single label. The muscadines have been relegated largely to their wines called Hostess or Mother Vineyard Scuppernong. In the 1970s, along with the Monarch Wine Company of Atlanta, the Sands' wineries put out the most widely sold vintages made from the *rotundifolia* grapes. The Mother Vineyard label was borne by more bottles called scuppernong than any rival.

At its outset in 1945 Canandaigua was primarily a supplier of bulk wines, but by 1972 when it went public, its growth had been phenomenal.[10] Its subsidiaries soon included Bisceglia Brothers in California, the Hammondsport Wine Company in New York, Tenner Brothers at Patrick, South Carolina, and the Richards Wine Cellars at Petersburg, Virginia. Both the southern plants produce peach and other fruit or berry wines as well as the scuppernong called Hostess (from Patrick) and Mother Vineyard (from Petersburg). Richards Wine Cellars, the largest winery in Virginia, derives a considerable portion of its muscadines from farms in North Carolina and is to a degree responsible for the recently renewed interest in grape growing in the state. It was established in 1951 as a kind of successor to the small Car-Cal Wine Company located in Greensboro, where Sallie Sands was once listed as owner. For a time the family apparently owned or controlled a vineyard in Moore County. The name Mother Vineyard became theirs in 1955. Twenty years earlier, as may be recalled, the Old Mother Vineyard at Manteo had agreed to dispose of its grapes to Paul Garrett.* As the Mother Vineyard brand of scuppernong flourished with the abundant success of the Sands family's enterprises, their Richards winery in Petersburg began to run short of the muscadines needed to maintain its flavor, and in 1961 they offered Carolina growers a free supply of plants and five-year contracts to purchase their grape harvests at $200 per ton. The New River Grape Growers Association and other vineyardists were thus stimulated. Raymond Hartsfield, who once maintained in Onslow County the only commercial winery in North Carolina, closed it in 1968, for he could do better financially, he thought, by merely raising grapes to ship to Virginia.†

In 1980 most of the wine made commercially from Carolina-grown muscadines was still produced outside the state, but there were a few newcomers to the thin ranks of Tarheel professional vintners. These have often consulted the experts in Raleigh, and, for whatever reasons, their wines are judged by many critics with delicate palates to be superior to the generally sweet and strong scuppernong sold by the much larger out-of-state producers. Two that call for special mention in these pages are the Wine Cellars, Inc. located in a historic neighborhood near Edenton and the Duplin Wine Cellars at Rose Hill, the latter situated in a region once world-famous for the growing of tuberoses.

The former uses the name Deerfield Vineyards for its products, its chief claim to fame being a dry table wine. Paul Williams, executive vice-president, handles the vinegrowing and the farming at the Deerfield grounds, the Wood Family at the Greenfield Vineyards. Their wines are made in the Red Barn, converted from tobacco storage, where visitors are welcomed. Planting was started in 1971 with scuppernong and Carlos grapes. Three years later the winery was ready, with a storage capacity of 13,000 gallons. Their blend of thirty percent of the juice of Delaware grapes from New York with that of their own muscadines results in "the best dry Scuppernong I have ever tasted," according to California expert Leon Adams.[11]

The Duplin Wine Cellars, with 40,000 gallons capacity, produces varietals and other quality beverages ranging from dry to sweet. It is a co-operative begun in 1970 by a group of farmers and local businessmen. Five years later they sold their first wines commercially, test-marketing

---

*Garrett in 1939 stated that the vineyard had been started about the time of the celebration of the 350th anniversary of the Lost Colony in order to exploit the "Mother Vine" at Manteo ("The Romance of American Wines," *America First*, II [Oct. 1939] 6).

†Hartsfield's father had started the winery at Holly Ridge in 1947 (Adams, pp. 46–47).

Old Mother Vineyard on Roanoke Island about 1930 (*courtesy Division of Archives and History, Raleigh, N.C.*)

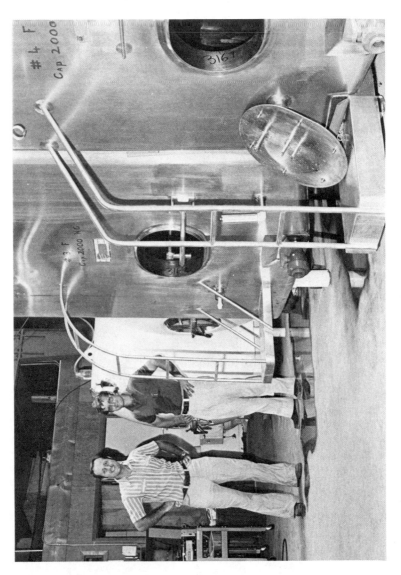

Steel fermentation tanks at Duplin Wine Cellars, Rose Hill, N.C. (*courtesy David Fussell*)

them in Wilmington, Raleigh, and Fayetteville. The next year they covered the state, sales being made in grocery stores, convenience markets, and wineshops. In 1979 they ventured across the border into South Carolina. Grapes are bought from members of the cooperative and others in a dozen or so counties, and are supposed to have been picked the same day they are delivered to the press. Their scuppernong is "one hundred percent Scuppernong," a great rarity indeed.[12] The Duplin *Tasting Guide*, for the use of visitors, who are welcomed Mondays through Fridays, lists the following:

Carolina Preeminence—dry table wine made from Carlos grapes, available as red or white;
Carolina Rose—medium-dry table wine, a blend of muscadines;
Noble—medium-dry wine made from dark muscadines of the Noble variety;
Carlos—medium-dry varietal;
Scuppernong—semi-sweet varietal;
Carolina Red—sweet blend, made according to "an old Southern recipe."

Both wineries report the scuppernong as their most popular vintage with customers.

The recent establishment in North Carolina of these and several other small wineries, of course, not only reflects to a degree a national trend but also marks a decided shift in political and other attitudes within the state. In June, 1965, the legislature in Raleigh stimulated research on the breeding, production, processing, and marketing of muscadine grapes specifically by assigning for such purposes $145,000 to the State Agricultural Experiment Station, to be used over a two-year period. The Agricultural Extension Service was similarly granted $21,000. According to the preamble of the enabling act,[13] farmers dependent on traditional crops like flue-cured tobacco stood in urgent need of supplementing their income, and grapes offered a potential recourse, especially since there existed "presently a large unfulfilled demand for wine made from North Carolina grapes to use in blends with other wines manufactured from less flavorful grapes produced in other parts of the country." The text further reads: "It is well known that the North Carolina grape has a delicate and extraordinary flavor." Mention was also made of the potential demand for fresh grapes in making "juices, jams, jellies, pasteurized soft drinks, and other food products." The proposed research was expected to deal with the breeding and evolution of new varieties of grapes as well as with the techniques of storing, freezing, concentrating, and fermenting their juice. Preservation of the distinctive flavor of the muscadines was specified as one of the ends to be sought in the "processed products," and close cooperation was anticipated among horticulturists, food scientists, agricultural economists, and specialists in extension education. One may interject here that the professors and experts in Raleigh and elsewhere responded quickly and ably to the opportunities presented by this carefully designed bill so long overdue.

In 1973 the solons who voted a state-wide referendum on "liquor by the drink" eased the tax burden on wines and winemakers from within the state and cleared the way further for such home vintners as made use of the so-called "wine-kits." Extension Horticultural Specialist Joe F. Brooks promptly alerted the agricultural agents: "These new laws clarify the statutes regarding wineries in the state, reduce the excise taxes on native wines to 5¢ per gallon, reduce the inventory taxes 40%, allow for host rooms at the winery, and reduce the annual winery license to $100."[14] Already in the spring of 1973, he added, a total of 900 acres of new vineyard plantings had been made, compared with 700 for 1972.

The Agricultural Extension Service in Raleigh had early responded to the General Assembly's funding of studies of the muscadines, and already in the autumn of 1965 issued a statement on financial prospects for farmers interested in growing the grapes for processing.[15] Its authors, Joe F. Brooks and Wallace Nave, mentioned the average price received during the period 1959–63 as $200 per ton but conservatively based their figures on half as much. Estimating harvests at five tons per acre and the cost of seasonal labor at a dollar an hour, they concluded, net revenue to land, operator's labor and management would amount to $306.37 per acre. The following year a broader study of *Economic Opportunities for Muscadine Grapes* appeared in the Extension Service's Information Series.[16] This survey, ably written by Gene Mathia, provided general information on various kinds of grapes, including the special virtues and handicaps of the muscadines, and on the existing state of the American wine industry as well as an appraisal of the likelihood of North Carolina growers making a profit. Producers in several southeastern counties, Mathia stated, had already asked questions about such prospects, and his concrete analysis of vineyard potential was confined to a four-county survey in that area. The state's grape industry, then in a "very rudimentary stage of development," he accurately judged, would have to depend largely on winemaking from muscadines, for which many more vineyards than presently existed would have to be planted with the new improved varieties to be expected from plant breeders already at work. Moreover, the muscadines, while not generally foxy in taste like other grapes grown in the eastern states, were nevertheless noted for producing wines strongly and distinctively flavored and lacking in uniformity. Such being the case, blending with other wines had been suggested as the best means of attaining uniformity.[17]*

Warning was also given that at the very moment concerted efforts were being made to generate efficient viniculture in North Carolina, grape growers in California and New York were facing a financial crisis. On the positive side, however, was increased Tarheel consumption of wines, estimated in 1964 as 2.4 million gallons, in quite a contrast to the beggarly 24 thousand produced in the state. The prices local growers received had risen to $183 per ton from $156 paid in 1963. If the price advanced to $175 a ton, Mathia believed, the smaller farmers might do better growing grapes rather than sweet potatoes, etc., and if the price settled down to $150 per ton and labor costs were calculated at $1.25 an hour "approximately 23 acres of grapes could be profitably produced on the farm unit containing 153 acres of cropland." Smaller acreages of cropland would fail to provide the farmer a profit from a vineyard. Among the several tables appended to Mathia's essay was one that gave the Wine Institute's estimates for per capita consumption of wine; a relevant portion is here presented:

National average	Year	North Carolina average
.855	1959	.301
.882	1960	.327
.904	1961	.383
.878	1962	.376
.907	1963	.416
.938	1964	.502

The need of a stimulus to local consumption spoke for itself.

Jumping ahead about a decade, to a time when the wine boom faintly foreshadowed in the table above registered visible effects all over the country, we turn to another study of the economic conditions of raising muscadines for processing in North Carolina. This one dates from July,

---

*In earlier days California's red wines particularly were criticized for their "earthy" taste. For that and other reasons, they were blended with Bordeaux shipped in bulk to the West Coast. Sometimes French labels had been attached (Henry Lachman, "Early California Wine Industry" [a paper prepared for the meeting of the International Congress of Viticulture held at the Panama-Pacific Exposition in July, 1915], *Official Report* [San Francisco, 1915], pp. 27–32).

1976, and limits its coverage to vineyards with grapes grown on single-wire trellises and harvested mechanically.[18] In harmony with the trend of the times, labor costs are estimated at $2.30 an hour. Reckoning on a price of $190 per ton, the study concludes, a vineyardist could expect returns to land, overhead, and management of $97.52 per acre, an ominous drop of $208.85 in a decade. Increased costs accompanied by the failure of grape prices to follow suit obviously dimmed prospects for farmers, many of whom have reported tobacco as more profitable.

The professors in Raleigh have also investigated the economics of establishing and operating a winery. In 1966 Gene Mathia and his colleagues prepared a preliminary survey which has been updated and expanded in a pamphlet published as Economic Information Report, No. 149.[19] According to the updated version, the production of muscadines in the state reached 2,000 tons in 1975, but demand from out-of-state wineries failed to progress. In-state plants, accordingly, might help to pick up the slack in the market and stimulate local consumption, especially since the protective tax on Carolina-produced wines would be a favorable factor. Cost analyses of wineries of three sizes (20, 100, and 500 thousand gallons capacity) disclosed the fact that a plant of small size could manufacture wine made solely from muscadines only at a cost of $1.86 per fifth and would need to purchase 20,000 gallons of bulk wine and blend it with its own vintages. For various reasons, including taxes, the most profitable winery would be that of medium size, which likewise would have to double its ultimate output by the use of bulk wines produced out of state. Wines from California and New York, cheaper in cost, could be blended with the muscadines about half and half without violating legal requirements for labeling.* Readers of the report who were contemplating a venture in commercial wine manufacture in North Carolina could perhaps take courage from hopes rather than convictions.

The home vintners were not overlooked in the flurry of recent publications bearing on grapes which have come from Raleigh, as will be evident to the amateur who secures a copy of the Agricultural Extension Service Bulletin No. 602, revised in 1978. It owes its merits largely to Daniel E. Carroll, a food specialist on the staff of North Carolina State University at Raleigh. He takes the novice step by step through the requisite procedures in a style marked by clear exposition and a talent for

---

*The *New York Times* in 1954 reported an Internal Revenue Service ruling to the effect that wines made from scuppernong grapes could be labeled as such or as muscadine but no red wine could be called scuppernong (Nov. 22, 1954).

simplifying without condescension. At the outset he warns the house-holder that 200 gallons may be made for home consumption, but a form must be filed with the Internal Revenue Service in advance. Professor Carroll recommends the old scuppernong along with several self-fertile cultivars developed in the state, two of them in cooperation with the federal Department of Agriculture. Their names, dates, and colors are: Tarheel (1948) black, Magnolia (1961) light bronze, Carlos (1970) bronze, Noble (1971) black. For making sparkling wine the Dixie (1976), a white grape, is also included as a leading variety.

The Home Economics Extension agents have also been helpful in cre-ating a market for fresh grapes by means of demonstrations and mimeo-graphed circulars. Collections of recipes for jellies, catsup, etc. often re-print formulas for wine, and of course syllabub, this last a traditional Christmas beverage automatically associated with the scuppernong in many southern families. More professionally, ingenious studies have been made in connection with a potential market for muscadines in northern supermarkets.[20] The results of the state's long-delayed effort to exploit the grapes await the verdict of time. No one can be sure in 1981 whether it is too little or too late.

CHAPTER VIII

The Scuppernong and the Plant Breeders

As the first chapters of this book have recorded, soon after the Big White Grape had been named by Dr. Calvin Jones, seeds of the scuppernong were eagerly planted here and there, and attempts were made to grow it, even in the North. At times promising seedlings were selected for cultivation, though many growers were discouraged by finding the fruits of their young vines purplish or black in color. Among the North Carolinians who persisted was Sidney Weller, the South's first wine man of note, who named one of his selections Weller's Halifax, sold vines liberally all over the region, and boasted in the 1850s that he had exhibited at the State Fair specimens of the fruit more than four inches in circumference. Louis Froelich at Kenansville likewise improved his grapes by breeding as well as by following methods of culture learned in the Rhineland. Early in the present century F. C. Reimer, a professional horticulturist employed by the state, undertook the first survey of surviving old vines and rounded up for study the several varieties of spontaneous muscadines then bearing names. In collaboration with L. R. Detjen, he next proceeded to scrutinize their pollination and actually reported a wild vine with perfect flowers, though not self-fertile.[1] About the same time, pomologists in Washington decided to undertake a broad investigation of all aspects of the muscadines, a venture which, as we have seen, led to collaboration with the North Carolina authorities, who put at the disposal of the experimenters the station maintained at Willard, in Pender County.

Outside North Carolina, of course, several others had been working with scuppernongs during the nineteenth century. Jarvis Van Buren, for example, had raised seedlings in batches of two thousand each from seeds planted successively at Clarkesville, Georgia, in 1867, 1868, and 1869. Of the first lot of his seedlings, only one bore white fruit; of the second, none; and of the third, three.[2] During this time, Van Buren brought out a little book in which he gathered up various recipes for winemaking and information largely derived from others.[3] Furthermore, in a widely disseminated manual by William N. White called *Gardening in the South*, he heartily recommended the scuppernong.[4]

In 1877 John McRae characterized his experiments with scuppernong seedlings in Camden County, South Carolina, as "amusing myself"—and gave his plants to his neighbors or to visitors.[5] Another South Carolinian, Dr. A. P. Wylie of Chester, was serious enough to warrant being recorded in the *Report of the American Pomological Society*, though his attempts to cross *vinifera* and *rotundifolia* were nugatory.[6] Far more important was Thomas V. Munson, who settled at Denison, Texas, in 1876 and not long thereafter achieved the rank of foremost authority on the native grapes of the United States. The species of muscadines represented by the so-called Mustang grape of Florida has been named for him, *Vitis munsoniana*. Munson's numerous experiments included crossing scuppernongs or other muscadines with the wild post oak grapes of the Texas region. Selections from these crosses were given names like San Jacinto, San Monta, and La Salle. They soon entered into the lineage of various cultivars later introduced by breeders working at the chief experimental centers. Most of the earliest grape breeding in the South was done by nurserymen or physicians, the usual purpose being to produce larger or sweeter fruit. In retrospect, all of it appears to have suffered from faulty techniques and today may seem like a groping in a geneless darkness rarely lighted even by the flickering glow of Mendel's findings, not to mention the illumination shed on the mechanisms of heredity by T. H. Morgan and his successors.

In 1913 the first general report from the federal pomologists on the cooperative studies at Willard and elsewhere confirmed Reimer's findings on the self-sterility of the scuppernong and its relatives but mentioned only briefly the on-going experiments with breeding the grapes.[7] Many years of testing were to pass before new varieties were named and introduced. Instead, an effort was made to "eliminate existing confusion" regarding the varieties already named in various quarters by providing descriptions of the "more promising ones." The scuppernong, of course, was ranked highest in "relative value" and headed the list, followed by the Flowers, James, Mish, and Thomas.* Of the total of twenty-one musca-

---

*The others were: Eden, Memory, Hopkins, Sugar, Carolina Belle, Beula, Luola, Smith, Lady James, Latham, Pee Dee, Tenderpulp, Clayton, Westbrook, Brown, and "San Jacinto and other hybrids." Reimer had also attempted a round-up of names.

dines listed, all save four originated in North Carolina; seven of them came from a radius of fifty miles embracing Whiteville, Lumberton, and Marion, South Carolina. Grapes and vines from five growers in Florida and more than a dozen in North Carolina were examined as well as those grown at Willard; and "at least three strains of light-colored Rotundifolia" were noted "among the cultivated varieties of Scuppernong grapes."[8]*

When the repeal of national Prohibition once again stirred the hopes of southern growers, the varieties of muscadines recommended were still the old standard ones. A special Farmers' Bulletin issued in 1938 by the federal government mentioned Munson's hybrids as merely "of interest chiefly to grape breeders" and brushed off new varieties developed by H. P. Stuckey in Georgia as too recent to have been sufficiently tested.[9]

But, in retrospect at least, it is clear that the University of Georgia had forged ahead in breeding the grapes. The site of its researches was an agricultural station appropriately named Experiment. The first two reports on its vineyard appeared in 1895 and 1901, when muscadines were only a few of the scores of different grapes growing there.† The second report did not fail to recommend as worthy the Thomas, Eden, and Flowers, along with quite an assortment of bunch grapes, and emphatically stated, "No home should be without an ample 'Scuppernong Arbor.'" The scuppernong had been one of the few of the several hundred varieties growing at the station which had recovered from a temperature of seven below zero recorded in February, 1899.[10] Special work with the muscadine was begun in Georgia as early as 1909, its researchers soon profiting by the reports from North Carolina prepared by Reimer and by the general survey issued in 1913 through the U.S. Department of Agriculture. At Experiment, Professor Stuckey and his staff chose the Thomas, the Flowers, and the scuppernong as female parents and pollinated them with four different grapes called merely Black Male Nos. 1 and 2 and White Male Nos. 1 and 2. Of the many seedlings resultant from these crosses six were deemed meritorious enough to warrant introduction by 1919, at which time a bulletin was issued on *Work with Vitis Rotundifolia.*[11] This reported the scuppernong "mother" as accounting for offspring named

---

*Could they have represented the old Tyrrell County stock, the Hickman, and the Roanoke? In 1934, J. G. Woodroof from Tifton, Georgia reported on "Five Strains of Scuppernong Variety of Muscadine Grape" (*Proceedings of the American Society for Horticultural Science*, XXXII [1934], 382–85).

†In 1919 the station reported 180 "Scuppernongs" then more than twenty years old. Two of these were still alive and bearing in 1979.

Dr. T. V. Munson (*courtesy Roy E. Renfro, Jr.,*
T. V. Munson Memorial Vineyard, Grayson
County College, Texas)

Old vine at Manteo about 1900 *(courtesy N. C. Museum of Natural History)*

Stuckey and November; the Thomas for Irene and Qualitas; and the Flowers for Spalding and Hunt. The last-mentioned was destined to become a continuing favorite. When the station issued a more general pamphlet on *Muscadine Grape Varieties and Culture* in 1931,[12] all of these six new grapes except Qualitas were recommended as the leading varieties, along with an older Georgia muscadine named Eden (originally discovered on a doctor's farm east of Atlanta), the Thomas from South Carolina, Munson's hybrid La Salle from Texas, and from North Carolina the Flowers, Memory, James, Mish, and scuppernong. Three of the older varieties as well as the Hunt, November, and Stuckey were starred as "best" for the home vineyard; rated highest in "eating quality" were the Hunt, Thomas, and scuppernong.[13] Obviously, the older standard varieties were then judged capable of surviving the competition—at least for the amateur grower.

Such apparently continued to be the case in Georgia as late as 1953, when M. M. Murphey issued a mimeographed statement on the development of new muscadines at Experiment. The scuppernong and Thomas, he observed, were "worthy of being retained," but the Hunt was the "best all-purpose" sort, though it fell short of the sweetness of such newer varieties as Topsail and Dulcet and lacked certain other qualities then being sought in the many seedlings still undergoing tests at the station.[14] When, however, in 1977 R. P. Lane "released" Georgia's nineteenth cultivar, named Summit,* its pedigree indicated none of the older names except Hunt and Irene, and these were three or four generations antecedent to the new grape.[15] These details indicate the quickened pace of breeding muscadines in an established center of experiment and the speed with which even fairly recent cultivars are often outmoded, not to mention the old standard grapes on which experimentation was originally based. We may now retrace our steps to the time when North Carolina recaptured its eminence in the history of the muscadines.

This took place about 1948 when Charles Dearing, a veteran horticulturist associated with the federal Bureau of Plant Industry, representing the cooperative venture at the Coastal Plain Branch of the North Carolina Agricultural Experiment Station, announced not only fifteen new varieties from the Willard tests but also among them the first perfect-flowered muscadines ever grown. A perfect-flowered plant is of course one whose blossom will yield fruit without dependence on another. At the

*Intended for the fresh fruit market, the Summit originated in a cross made in 1965 by B. O. Fry, the seedling having been selected in 1971.

time, the recommended practice in commercial vineyards was to set out at least one male plant for every ten bearers; the substitution of the new perfect-flowered discoveries would thus increase yields by ten percent or more. Because this advance was of signal importance more detail concerning its inception may be in order.

Soon after 1905, when the pomologists in Washington decided to make a general study of the South's chief grape, seeds from Munson's crosses in Texas were secured, and at New Smyrna, Florida, the scuppernong, James, Thomas, and Flowers were crossed with several of the local native vines, one of which was named Mission because it was found clambering over an old Spanish ruin. The seeds from the Florida crosses and those from Munson were germinated and grown at the Arlington, Virginia, experimental grounds in 1908 and 1909, and the resultant seedlings were then transferred to the vineyard plots at Willard. After the vines blossomed and fruited there, the better ones were again crossed, with standard varieties or with other outstanding seedlings, or with local varieties found through new field surveys throughout the Southeast, or with certain wild male plants. Again selections were made for further breeding. Moreover, from New York, New Jersey, and California pollen of bunch grapes, native and foreign in origin, was shipped for use at Willard and other participating vineyards in the South, but such hybrids as resulted were deemed of little promise, and more extended work with them was abandoned. The objective, Dearing stated, was the production of perfect-flowered sorts possessed of good quality and of varieties with higher sugar content, thinner skins, better pulp characteristics, smaller seeds, and larger clusters.[16] Winemaking was not a clearly defined goal; in fact, at the beginning in 1905 the suggestion had been made that since local Prohibition laws were driving southern wineries out of business the government would do well to help farmers owning vineyards to find new outlets for their grapes.

In 1911 when the first seedlings planted at Willard put out flowers, a careful inspection disclosed one solitary specimen that indicated hermaphroditic potentiality. This came from a group of forty-four seedlings representing a cross between the old Georgia Eden and the newly named Mission from Florida. The next year, when additional young plants bloomed for the first time, a painstaking check turned up a second perfect-flowered specimen, this one from a batch of seven crosses of a scuppernong female with a white staminate from New Smyrna. It was better than the first because it fruited more easily in the bags protecting its clusters from insects. In color and general appearance the berries looked much like those of its mother vine. From these two starts hundreds of perfect-flowered muscadines were soon raised, but the first forty years' work at Willard yielded only two others of distinctly different parentage that ever showed the same hermaphroditic characteristics—and they were so inferior as to be eventually discarded.

The fifteen varieties announced by Dearing in 1948 were as follows: {D = dark-fruited; W = light-fruited; P = perfect flowers]:

(DP) Burgaw	Cross of Thomas pollinated by second perfect-flowered grape.
(W) Cape Fear	Cross of Burgaw with a cross of first perfect-flowered grape.
(D) Creswell	Discovered on the farm of F. R. White at Creswell.
(DP) Duplin	Cross of Stanford [see below].
(W) Kilgore	Seedling of Munson's San Jacinto. Named for a former director of the station.
(W) Morrison	Cross of scuppernong with a white staminate seedling. Named for Governor Cameron Morrison.
(W) New River	Seedling grown at Arlington from a scuppernong furnished by Munson.
(D) Onslow	Cross of a white-fruited seedling with pollen from Burgaw.
(W) Orton	Cross of Latham (a natural seedling found near New Bern) with Burgaw.
(WP) Pender	Cross of Latham with a white-fruited, perfect-flowered seedling.
(W) Stanford	Cross of San Jacinto. Named for J. A. Stanford, a citizen of Willard.
(DP) Tarheel	Cross of Luola (found near Lumberton) with a perfect-flowered selection.
(W) Topsail	Cross of Latham and Burgaw. "Unanimously rated as having a better flavor than Scuppernong." Pearly-green rather than bronze in color.
(WP) Wallace	Cross with Willard [see below]. James, Eden, and a native male vine were in its parentage.
(WP) Willard	Cross of two white-colored seedlings propagated at Arlington.

Most of these varieties bearing white fruit had the scuppernong somewhere in their ancestry.

With the benefit of the perfect-flowered varieties and the subsequent heightened interest in wines, the breeding of muscadines has sped merrily on its way. Older names have dropped out as newer ones are introduced from the experiment stations of the federal government or the several land-grant colleges interested. In California the muscadines have long since been used not only by the breeders of improved root stocks but also by those seeking to hybridize them with the *vinifera*. The U.S. Department of Agriculture has continued its interest with happy results. The Albemarle (Topsail × Burgaw), for example, was jointly announced by North Carolina and federal researchers in 1961, the same year that they introduced Magnolia (Topsail × Tarheel). And while the professors at the state university in Raleigh and at the University of Georgia continue excellent work, largely on the bases established by predecessors in their local experiment stations, they are joined by colleagues in Florida, Mississippi, and elsewhere.[17] Collaboration among the grape experimenters has brought about excellent results. For example the new variety called Dixie was introduced in 1976 by both the North Carolina and Florida experiment stations, and in 1979 a dark muscadine named Regale was jointly released by the men in Raleigh and those at Mississippi State. Approximately where the old scuppernong stands, after two hundred years and the latter-day excitement of breeding new rivals galore, may be glimpsed in the pedigree of Dixie on the following page.

The dramatic developments in improving the muscadines owing to federal and state experimenters and observable during the past few decades are among the highlights of recent American viticulture and, provided proper encouragement is offered, give promise of continuing. A muscadine of quite a range in color, sweeter than any previously known, of a size larger than that of a golf ball, with a dry stem scar, fewer and smaller seeds, or indeed with none at all, is well within reasonable expectation for the fresh-fruit market. If proper backing is assured, whatever qualities are needed to improve the existing wine varieties among the *rotundifolia* are likely to be obtained. And the crossing of the species with the *vinifera*, heralded by recent successes at Davis, California, and elsewhere, may open a new vista on winemaking in the South if a market for Dixie-made wines can be developed. But, obviously, the Big White Grape will continue to fade into the background as the new cultivars multiply. The adjective Big is now a misnomer. The scuppernong has long since lost its rating for size. The Jumbo, Higgins, Fry,* and others have relegated it to the "medium-size" category, as has also Professor

---

*B. O. Fry, one of the chief developers of large-sized muscadines, mentioned the potency of a "white male" pollinator thought to have been a scuppernong ("Value of Certain Varieties and Selections in the Breeding of High Quality, Large-fruited Muscadine Grapes," *American Journal for Horticultural Science*, XCI [Dec., 1907], 214).

PEDIGREE OF DIXIE

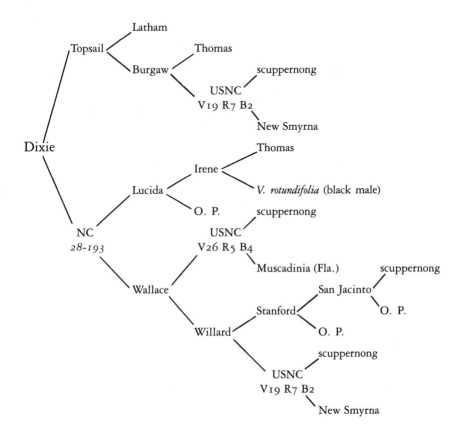

Source: W. B. Nesbitt and W. H. Underwood, "'Dixie' Grape," *HortScience*, XI (Oct., 1976), 521.
O. P. means open pollinated.

W. B. Nesbitt's 1979 introduction named Sterling, a bronze muscadine with berries larger than those of any previous perfect-flowered cultivar. The scuppernong "shatters" from the vine and has other faults; its percentage of sugar in the free run of juice is lower than that of Dixie, Albemarle, and others, yet the old grape has not joined Model T in the graveyard of rejects. Its past momentum carries it on to a degree. Witness the *Muscadine Grape Production Guide for North Carolina*, revamped in 1978,[18] where it is listed among the eleven "currently most important" of the dozens of named varieties.* And the federal Farmers' Bulletin on the grapes, in its 1973 avatar, likewise listing "eleven important muscadine grape varieties," honors the old favorite by inclusion.[19] The Bulletin also gives warning that "many different selections have been propagated as Scuppernong. Most of those being propagated by the better nurserymen are superior bronze grapes, although they may not be from the original Scuppernong."

Whether original or not, a vine or two called scuppernong is still standard with home growers in many areas of the South. As for its survival in commercial vineyards, one can be more exact, at least so far as North Carolina is concerned. Following is a digest of the results of a survey made in 1976 by the state's Crop and Livestock Service.[20] Commercial growers in North Carolina numbered 282 at the end of 1976, up from 115 in 1968 and 231 in 1972, positive evidence of a rise in interest reflecting the nation's wine boom. Of all the counties Onslow had the largest number of vineyards (25), followed by Cleveland (14), Johnston (13), Jones and Lenoir (12 each), and Bladen (11). These six counties contributed nearly a third of the state's total. The acreage involved likewise indicated a boomlet. The 2494 acres reported for 1976 statewide were up 47 percent over the 1,677 recorded in 1972 and represented more than four times the area in commercial vineyards in 1968. Though Cleveland County was foremost with 315 acres, the coastal plains accounted for 70 percent of the area in vines in 1976. Muscadines made up 96 percent of North Carolina grape plantings, bunch varieties like Concord or Niagara 3.5 percent, and the new and highly touted French-American hybrids a picayune .05 percent.† The leading grape (nearly 47

---

*The others are Albemarle, Carlos, Cowart, Dixie, Noble, Fry, Higgins, Hunt, Magnolia, and Tarheel.

†So far, North Carolina's chief connection with the French hybrids seems to have been associated with the variety called Aurora, which was introduced to American commercial vineyardists in 1946 by Philip Wagner of Riderwood, Maryland, an amateur now credited with altering the course of winemaking in the eastern states. Originally, the Aurora was given to Professor R. T. Dunstan,

percent) was the Carlos, introduced in 1970 by the North Carolina Agricultural Experiment Station. It is similar to the scuppernong but perfect-flowered. Ranked second in acreage planted (20 percent) was the Magnolia, another bronze-colored cultivar. The scuppernong was third with 12 percent. These three varieties made up almost 80 percent of the state's total acreage.* Devotees of the old grape may find consolation in the fact that both the Carlos and the Magnolia have the scuppernong in their background by way of the Topsail and the Burgaw, but the small satisfaction thus derived would be like boasting: "Great-grandpa once owned that beautiful vineyard over there."

Of course, a plant as noted for longevity as the scuppernong does not disappear in a hurry. And for most of those who like the wine made from its fruit there is something very fascinating in its special flavor that other muscadines do not possess. The Duplin Wine Cellars in Rose Hill reports the scuppernong still the most popular of its varietals, accounting for more than half of the cooperative's total sales.[21] F. C. Reimer, the chief early historian of the grape, in 1909 set forth his opinion that this rich, light-colored wine had no superior among the sweet wines of the nation, praise that continues to be echoed in many quarters of the South. But perhaps a special nostalgic factor enters into the rating. As Alabama's Rose Reynolds remarked in prefacing instructions on how to make the genuine, old-fashioned vintage, "Now don't look to this not to fail if you don't do like I tell you. And when I've done told you all I know, then, you still gotta have a sort o' feelin' about it, and if you ain't got that feelin,' you just as good go buy your wine someres. . . ."[22] Really to appreciate the scuppernong perhaps one may need to have that "sort o' feelin'." Without it the old grape will in time probably disappear from its native scene.

---

then of Greensboro College, who in turn forwarded cuttings to Wagner. Professor Dunstan's interest may be glimpsed in his article "Hybridization of *Euvitis* × *Vitis rotundifolia*: Back Crosses to Muscadine" (*Proceedings of the American Society for Horticultural Science*, LXXXIV [June, 1964], 238–42).

*Other varieties of muscadines planted were the Higgins and Fry (white) and Noble and Hunt (dark). The Noble, introduced in 1971 by North Carolina breeders (Thomas × Tarheel), is considered the best of its sort for making red wine.

Source Notes

1. *The Early History of the Grape*

1. *Sketches of Lower North Carolina* (Raleigh, N.C., 1861), p. 52.
2. *The Colonial Records of North Carolina*, ed. W. L. Saunders (Raleigh, N.C., 1886), I, 766.
3. Ibid., 766, 770.
4. Ibid., XXII, 509; XXIII, 150; XXIV, 861.
5. The first volume of the Pettigrew papers (Raleigh, N.C., 1971) was edited by Sarah M. Lemmon, who has also provided a biography of *Parson Pettigrew of the "Old Church," 1744–1807* (Chapel Hill, N.C., 1970).
6. W. R. Gerard, in *Handbook of American Indians North of Mexico*, ed. F. W. Hodge (Washington, D.C., 1910), Part II, 493.
7. *A Brief and True Report of the New Found Land of Virginia*, with an Introduction by R. G. Adams (New York, 1951), Part III.
8. *The Natural History of North Carolina* (Dublin, 1737), p. 73.
9. Ibid., p. 92. Brickell's discussion of the native grapes, like much else in his book, derives in part from John Lawson, *A New Voyage to Carolina* (1718), of which the best edition was prepared by Hugh Lefler (Chapel Hill, N.C., 1967).
10. Josiah Quincy, *Memoir of the Life of Josiah Quincy, Jr. . . . 1744–1775*, 2d ed. (Boston, 1874), pp. 95, 86.
11. P. 38.
12. U.S. Dept. of Agriculture, Special Report No. 36 (Washington, D.C., 1880).
13. P. 85.
14. N.C. Agriculture Experiment Station Bulletin 201.
15. Pp. 7, 10.
16. Leon D. Adams, *The Wines of America*, 2d ed. (New York, 1978), pp. 49, 69. All subsequent references, except where specified, are to this edition.
17. (Washington, D.C., 1850), pp. 283-86. The federal reports on agriculture were issued as part of the duties of the Patent Office until 1862.
18. IX (July 20, 1827), 139-40.
19. (New York, 1830), pp. 167-69.
20. *American Farmer*, IX (April 13, 1827), 29.
21. Ibid., X (March 21, 1828), 4.
22. *Southern Agriculturalist*, II (Nov., 18298), 499–501.
23. Reimer, p. 7.
24. *Biographical Directory of the Governors of the U.S. 1789–1975*, ed. R. Sobel and J. Raino (Westport, Conn., 1978), III, 1123.
25. III, 323-33.
26. In addition to the *Dictionary of American Biography*, for a fuller account see Marshall D. Haywood's article in the *North Carolina Booklet*, XIX (July–Oct., 1919), 3-35. Cf. also Thomas B. Jones, "Calvin Jones, M.D.: A Case Study in the Practice of Early American Medicine," *North Carolina Historical Review*, XLIX (Jan., 1972), 56-71; and Merle Curti, *The American Peace Crusade, 1815–1860* (Durham, N.C., 1929), p. 32.
27. *American Farmer*, X (Nov. 7 and 14, 1828), 265-66, 273-74.
28. Oct. 12, 1809; March 8, 1810; Sept. 13, 1810.
29. U. P. Hedrick, *A History of Horticulture in America to 1860* (New York, 1950), p. 432.
30. In addition to the sketches in the *Dictionary of American Biography*, see the annals of horticulture such as Hedrick, *A History of Horticulture in America to 1860*; and Christine C. Robbins, *David Hosack: Citizen of New York* (Philadelphia, 1964).
31. I have been unable to identify this work, which may never have survived the planning stage.

32. J. T. Scharf and T. Westcott, *History of Philadelphia* (Philadelphia, 1884), I, 511.

33. (Philadelphia, 1807), p. 304. Mease's interest in vines and wines is best seen in the lengthy articles on these topics in A. T. M. Willich's *Domestic Encyclopædia*, the American edition of which he edited, in five volumes (Philadelphia, 1804).

34. March 28, 1811. Blount's letter bears the date March 8, 1811.

35. *Raleigh Star*, Feb. 21, 1811.

36. William Prince, *A Treatise on the Vine* (New York, 1830), pp. 165-66.

37. *American Agriculturist*, IV (1845), 179.

38. R. C. Garlick, *Philip Mazzei, Friend of Jefferson* (Baltimore, 1933), pp. 43–47. Mazzei's recollections of his Virginia experiences appear in translation in *William and Mary College Quarterly*, IX (July, 1929), 160-74.

39. *American Farmer*, III (Jan. 11, 1822), 330.

40. *The Family Letters of Thomas Jefferson*, ed. E. M. Betts and J. A. Bear, Jr. (Columbia, Mo., 1966), pp. 446-48.

41. *The Writings of Thomas Jefferson*, Memorial Edition (Washington, D.C., 1904), XVIII, 318-20.

42. *American Farmer*, VIII (Oct. 6, 1826), 227.

43. Ibid., VII, 45.

44. Ibid., VII (April 29, 1825), 45.

45. See the *American Farmer*, VII (May 6, 1825), 55 for the possums, etc. The sketch in the *Dictionary of American Biography* is based largely on the ampler one published in *The Plough, the Loom, and the Anvil*, VII (July, 1854), 1–20.

46. The general nature of the farm journal is set forth in Albert L. Demaree, *The American Agricultural Press, 1819–1860*. Cf. also W. H. Wallace, "North Carolina's Agricultural Journals, 1838–1861; A Crusading Press," *North Carolina Historical Review*, XXXVI (July, 1957), 275–306.

47. C. O. Cathey lists the earliest North Carolina farm journals in his valuable survey of *Agricultural Developments in North Carolina 1783–1860* (Chapel Hill, N.C., 1956), pp. 84-85, and presents a neat account of Weller in "Sidney Weller: Ante-Bellum Promoter of Agricultural Reform," *North Carolina Historical Review*, XXXI (Jan., 1954), 1-17.

48. *DeBow's Review*, IV (June, 1848), 310–18.

49. Report of the Commissioner of Patents (Washington, D.C., 1854), Part II, 306-9.

50. VI (Sept., 1848), 200-204.

51. A typical example is "The Costs of Southern Vineyards," *DeBow's*, VIII (March, 1850), 245-49.

52. Hedrick, pp. 494-95.

53. For example, in the *Southern Agriculturist*, II (March, 1829), 148.

54. *Horticulturist*, VI (1851), 11-14, 243-44; *American Agriculturist*, X (1851), 304-5.

55. Wilmington *Commercial*, Sept. 8, 1849.

56. *Commercial*, Aug. 11, 1849, and reprinted in several later issues.

57. (Washington, D.C., 1852), Part II, pp. 48-51.

58. *Farmers' Journal*, I (1852), 193-94.

59. U.S. Patent Office, Report of the Commissioner of Patents (Washington, D.C., 1858), Part II, 227-32. The general plan of the investigation is explained in the Report for 1861, Part II, 4. For the importance of Le Conte and his family, after whom a famous pear was named, see Hedrick, pp. 282-83.

60. U.S. Patent Office, *Report on the Saccharine Contents of Native American Grapes in Relation to Winemaking*, Report of the Commissioner of Patents for the Year 1859 (Washington, D.C., 1860), Part II, 42-61.

61. *A Memoir of the Cultivation of the Vine in America and the Best Mode of Making Wine*, 2d ed. (Washington, D.C., 1828), p. 176.

62. For the introduction of the Catawba see, e.g., George Husmann, *The Cultivation of the Native Grape* (New York, 1870); and L. H. Bailey, *Sketch of the Evolution of Our Native Fruits*, pp. 50ff.

63. F. C. Reimer, *Scuppernong and other Muscadine Grapes*, N.C. Agricultural Experiment Station Bulletin No. 201 (Raleigh, N.C., 1909); and Charles Dearing, *Muscadine Grapes*, U.S. Department of Agriculture Farmers' Bulletin, No. 1785 (Washington, D.C., 1938).

64. T. S. Memory supplied the details in the *Southern Cultivator*, XXV (1877) 29; Reimer, pp. 14, 16. A muscadine was also named for Memory. Cf. also Memory's letter in the *Carolina Farmer*, I (February, 1869), 113-14.

65. Reimer, p. 14.

II. *Wines and Vines in the Old North State*

1. Ms. Collection, Duke University Library, Durham, N.C.
2. *Transactions of the North-Carolina State Agricultural Society for 1858* (Raleigh, N.C., 1859), pp. 10–13.
3. *Grape Culturist,* II (Feb., 1870), 38; II (July, 1870), 174–77.
4. Leon D. Adams, *The Wines of America*, pp. 82–83.
5. Ibid., 40.
6. For a historical sketch, see J. A. Lineback, *Thirteenth Annual Report of the North Carolina Horticultural Society* (Raleigh, N.C., 1893).
7. *Progressive Farmer*, I (Aug. 11, 1886), 4.
8. *Carolina Farmer*, I (July, 1869), 274. See also J. Van Buren, *Cultivator and Country Gentleman*, XXVI (Aug. 24, 1871), 335.
9. George C. Husmann and Charles Dearing, *The Muscadine Grape*, U.S. Department of Agriculture Bureau of Plant Industry Bulletin, No. 273 (Washington, D.C., 1913), pp. 54–55.
10. I. J. Isaacs, *The City of Wilmington* (Wilmington, N.C., 1912), p. 95. See also *Wilmington Up-to-date* (Wilmington, N.C., 1902), pp. 58–59, 69, 104.
11. Bulletin (Raleigh, N.C., 1887), p. 9.
12. *North Carolina State Directory 1877–78* (Fayetteville, N.C., 1877).
13. John A. Oates, *The Story of Fayetteville*, 2d ed. (Fayetteville, N.C., 1950), p. 538.
14. See, for example, Vincent P. Carosso, *The California Wine Industry 1830–1895* (Berkeley, Calif., 1951), pp. 152–59.
15. W. J. Green, "Essay on American Grape Culture," *Historical and Descriptive Review of the State of North Carolina* (Charleston, S.C., 1885) I, 42–50. For sketches of McBuie and Green, see ibid., 156–58; reprinted in Green's promotional booklet, *Tokay Vineyard, Near Fayetteville, N.C.* (Boston, 188[?]). See also *Raleigh News and Observer* for Aug. 7, 1910.
16. *Food and Adulteration: Speech of Hon. Wharton J. Green* (Washington, D.C., 1884), p. 7.
17. *Progressive Farmer*, II (May 19, 1887), 1.
18. *Report of the North Carolina State Horticultural Society, 1885* (Raleigh, N.C., 1886).
19. *Hand-Book of North Carolina* (Raleigh, N.C., 1893), pp. 257–58.
20. *North Carolina Planter*, II (Nov., 1859), 323–25, 309.
21. *The Scuppernong Grape* (Raleigh, N.C., 1913), p. 15.
22. N.C. Dept of Agriculture, Experiment Station Bulletin, No. 129 (July 10, 1896).
23. Ibid., No. 72 (June 1, 1890), pp. 3–10.
24. XXI (1906), 4; see also Husmann and Charles Dearing, *The Muscadine Grape*; Farmer's Bulletin, No. 709 (April 1, 1916); the annual reports of the Secretary of the Department of Agriculture for 1913, 1917, and 1919 give the general findings.
25. U.S. Dept of Agriculture, *Southern Fruit-Growing for Market*, Report of the Commissioner, 1871, (Washington, D.C., 1872), p. 149.
26. *Reminiscences of the Past Sixty Years* (Charlotte, N.C., 1908), p. 187.
27. *Southern Fruit-Growing for Market*, pp. 148–53.
28. *Roanoke News*, Sept. 28, 1893.
29. See, for example, the Atlanta-based *Plantation*, I (Jan. 22, 1870), 4; reprinted from the *Rural Carolinian*. The Agriculture Department's report for 1871 outlined his suggestions, *Southern Fruit-Growing for Market*, pp. 149–53.
30. Cf. also Husmann and Dearing, *The Muscadine Grape*, pp. 59–60.

III. *The Garretts*

1. C. W. Garrett & Co., *Price List* (Medoc, N.C., n.d.). Copy kindly furnished by Mrs. Louis McG. Hall of Chapel Hill.
2. IV (Oct., 1872), 301–2.
3. Dictated ms., pp. 48–51.
4. N. C. Dept. of Agriculture, *Experiment Station Report* (Raleigh, N. C., 1911), p. 118.
5. *Roanoke News*, June 22, 1893.
6. Ibid., Dec. 13, 1894.
7. Dictated ms., p. 55.
8. Francis B. Simkins, *The Tillman Movement in South Carolina* (Durham, N.C., 1926), chap. 8;

John E. Eubanks, *Ben Tillman's Baby: The Dispensary System of South Carolina 1892–1915* (Augusta [?], Ga., 1950).

9. Dictated ms., pp. 79–80.
10. *Official Catalogue of Exhibitors* (St. Louis, 1904).
11. The Library of Congress lists only one surviving copy—in the Alderman Library at the University of Virginia.
12. Philadelphia: privately printed by J. B. Lippincott, 1901.
13. *The Art of Serving Wine*, pp. 24–34.
14. Adams, 1st ed. (Boston, 1973), pp. 44–45. "Billionaire" was changed in later printings.

IV. *Prohibition*

1. U. S. Tariff Commission, *Grapes, Raisins, & Wines*, Annual Report, 2d Series, No. 134 (Washington, D.C., 1939), p. 232. Hereinafter cited as *Tariff Report No. 134*. Many previously published statistics are conveniently reprinted in it.
2. Clark Warburton, *The Economic Results of Prohibition* (New York, 1932), p. 35. These figures are extrapolated estimates. Cf. also *Tariff Report No. 134*, p. 391.
3. "Twentieth Century Supplement," *Norfolk Virginian-Pilot*, June, 1900.
4. *Progressive Farmer*, XXII (Jan. 23, 1908), 8.
5. Daniel J. Whitener, *Prohibition in North Carolina, 1715–1945* (Chapel Hill, N.C., 1946), p. 23.
6. *The Anti-Saloon League Year Book 1919*, ed. Ernest H. Cherrington (Westerville, Ohio, 1919), p. 205.
7. *The Anti-Saloon League Year Book 1920* (Westerville, Ohio, 1920).
8. *Raleigh News and Observer*, Jan. 8 and 16, 1914.
9. Whitener, p. 150.
10. *Standard Encyclopedia of the Alcohol Problem* (Westerville, Ohio, 1929), V, 2007.
11. Whitener, p. 53.
12. Broadside, Casper Company, ca. 1898, in Duke University Library Ms. Collection.
13. Broadside, Old Nick Whiskey Co., 1890, in Duke University Ms. Collection. Old Nick is recalled by erstwhile Chapel Hill student Peter M. Wilson, *Southern Exposure* (Chapel Hill, N.C., 1927), p. 37.
14. H. G. Crowgey, *Kentucky Bourbon* (Lexington, Ky., 1971), chap. 7.
15. *Anti-Saloon League Year Book 1909* (Columbus. Ohio, 1909), pp. 242–43. The 1919 *Year Book of the U.S. Brewers' Association* ([New York, 1920], pp. 173–74) also listed such medicines and their potency.
16. Thomas M. Coffey, *The Long Thirst: Prohibition in America: 1920–1933* (New York, 1975), p. 7.
17. Mabel W. Willebrandt, *The Inside of Prohibition* (Indianapolis, Ind., 1929), p. 90.
18. U. S. Revenue Service, *Statistics Concerning Intoxicating Liquors* (Washington, D. C., 1933).
19. *Annual Report of the President of the Association Against the Prohibition Amendment* (New York, 1932).
20. *Eastern North Carolina: The Land of Opportunity: The Home of the Scuppernong Grape: Southern Vineyard Company* (Philadelphia, ca. 1905), pp. 6, 17.
21. Pp. 26–28.
22. U. S. Treasury Dept., *Statistics Covering Intoxicating Liquors* (1922, 1933).
23. Clark Warburton, *The Economic Results of Prohibition* (New York, 1932), chap. 2.
24. Ibid., p. 165.
25. *New York Times*, Nov. 21, 1920.
26. Warburton, p. 157.
27. *Fortune*, IV (Oct., 1931), 54–55 (map).
28. *Tariff Report, No. 134*, p. 367.
29. H. L. Mencken and R. I. McDavid, *The American Language* (New York, 1963), pp. 208–9.

V. *Wine Concentrates and "Home Manufacture"*

1. IX, 44ff. Cited later as *Fortune*.
2. Adams, pp. 398–99.
3. Dictated ms., copy in Duke University Library.

4. Thomas M. Coffey, p. 187.
5. *Fortune*, 51, 118; Adams, p. 29; U. S. Tariff Comm., *Grapes, Raisins & Wines*, pp. 62 ff.; Gilman M. Ostrander, *The Prohibition Movement in California, 1848–1933* (Berkeley, Calif., 1957), chap. 10; Coffey, pp. 264–65, 289–91.
6. Ostrander, p. 179.
7. *New York Times*, Sept. 30, 1930, p. 28.
8. Ibid., Aug. 10, 1931, p. 6.
9. Coffey, pp. 289–90.
10. *The Mirrors of 1932* (New York, 1931), pp. 242–43. See also Coffey, pp. 76 ff.
11. Ostrander, p. 180.
12. Ibid.
13. *Federal Reporter Second Series* (St. Paul, Miss., 1932), LIII (2), 220.
14. Ibid., pp. 231, 239.
15. *Fortune*, VII (May, 1933), 8.
16. *New York Times*, April 28, 1932, p. 15.
17. Ostrander, p. 180.
18. Adams, pp. 400, 411, 460–61.
19. *Fortune*, 118.

VI. *Post-Repeal*

1. M. A. Amerine and V. L. Singleton, *Wine: An Introduction*, 2d ed. (Berkeley, Calif., 1977), pp. 288–89; Adams, pp. 35 et passim.
2. Adams, pp. 124 et seq.
3. Paul Garrett, *Wine as an American Industry* (n. pl., 1935 [?]), p. 12.
4. Interviews of importance are included in "The Wines of the U.S.," *Fortune*, IX (Feb., 1934), 44 et seq. and the *New York Times*, Nov. 4, 1935. His own circulars or pamphlets are *Wine as an American Industry*, cited above, *Notes on Wine and Its Service* (New York, 1934), and *Viticulture in the U.S. and Especially in the South* (n. pl., 1935 [?]).
5. P. 15.
6. P. 6.
7. *Viticulture in the U.S.*, pp. 3–4.
8. Frank Freidel, *Launching the New Deal*, Vol. IV of *Franklin D. Roosevelt* (Boston, 1973), chap. 6. See also George B. Tindall, *The Emergence of the New South 1913–1945*, Vol. X of *A History of the South* (Baton Rouge, La., 1967), chaps. 10 and 11.
9. Freidel, p. 84.
10. Tindall, p. 409.
11. *Pioneering in Rural Habilitation in North Carolina*, ed. Walter Cutter (Raleigh, N.C., 1935).
12. Ibid., p. 49.
13. I, 26.
14. *Raleigh News and Observer*, Aug. 15, 1937, p. 12.
15. Adams, p. 52.
16. *North Carolina: A Guide to the Old North State* (Chapel Hill, N.C., 1939), pp. 494–95.

VII. *Recent Effervescence*

1. *Public Laws of North Carolina, 1935*, chap. 393, p. 606. For the Turlington Act and subsequent developments, see Daniel J. Whitener, *Prohibition in North Carolina, 1715–1945* (Chapel Hill, N.C., 1945), chaps. 12 and 14.
2. Conditions in California during the period immediately following Repeal are outlined in *Grapes, Raisins & Wines*, pp. 65ff.
3. March 20, 1940. Garrett's letter had been printed on November 8, 1935.
4. *New York Times*, April 2, 1943, p. 29; Jan. 14, 1944, p. 22.
5. Ibid., Dec. 20, 1949.
6. May 3, 1973, p. 1.
7. Hawthorne Books as quoted in the *Wall Street Journal*, Oct. 28, 1971, p. 1.
8. Press release of Garrett and Company, ca. 1946. Copy in the Garrett file in the library of the Wine Institute in San Francisco.
9. *Corona Independent*, Sept. 16, 1952.

10. For the history of Canadaigua Wine Company, as it is now called, see Adams, pp. 143–44; Standard and Poor's *OTC Stock Reports*; and Philip Hiaring, "Canandaigua a Success Story," *Wines & Vines*, Sept. 1971, pp. 47–52.

11. P. 54. Frank C. Williams has provided the information not available from the various advertising folders issued by the winery.

12. Information provided by Ann Fussell.

13. *Session Laws of North Carolina*, chap. 1065, pp. 1484–87.

14. Mimeographed circular headed *The Muscadine Grape Situation* (Fall, 1973). Cf. *Session Laws 1973*, chap. 316; *1975*, chap. 722; *1977*, chap. 676.

15. *Horticultural Information Leaflet*, No. 203 (Nov., 1965).

16. No. 128 (Sept., 1966).

17. P. 8.

18. Mimeographed sheet supplied in advance of publication by Ed. Estes, economist, North Carolina State University, Jan. 28, 1980.

19. *Economic Opportunities for Profitable Winery Operations in North Carolina* (Raleigh, N.C., 1977).

20. E. A. Proctor, *Muscadine Grape Fresh Market Study* (Raleigh, N.C., 1979). A good example of a collection of recipes is *From the Vine*, compiled by Mrs. Chase C. Padgett of Onslow County (n.pl., n.d.).

VIII. *The Scuppernong and the Plant Breeders*

1. F. C. Reimer and L. R. Detjen, *Self-sterility of the Scuppernong and Other Muscadines* and *Breeding Muscadine Grapes*, N.C. Agricultural Experiment Station Bulletin, No. 209 (Sept., 1910) and No. 210 (May, 1914).

2. *Southern Cultivator*, XXX (Jan., 1872), 69–70.

3. *The Scuppernong Grape: Its History and Mode of Cultivation* (Memphis, 1868).

4. (New York, 1868), pp. 374–76.

5. *American Farmer*, N.S. VI (Feb., 1877), 62.

6. "Hybridization of Rotundifolia Grapes," *Proceedings for 1868*, XIII, 113–16. Cf. also *Proceedings for 1871*; and Marshall P. Wilder, *Lecture on the Hybridization of Plants . . .* (Boston, 1872), pp. 14–15.

7. Husmann and Dearing, *The Muscadine Grape*, pp. 41–43. For more detail, see also Dearing, "Muscadine Grapes," *Journal of Heredity*, VIII (Aug., 1917), 409–24.

8. Husmann and Dearing, p. 44.

9. Charles Dearing, *Muscadine Grapes*, U.S. Dept. of Agriculture Farmer's Bulletin, No. 1785 (Jan., 1938), p. 1.

10. A. L. Quaintance, *Second Report on Grapes*, Georgia Experiment Station Bulletin, No. 53 (June, 1901), pp. 52, 59.

11. Bulletin, No. 133 (Dec. 1919).

12. J. G. Woodroof and J. E. Bailey, Circular, No. 94 (Dec., 1931).

13. Bulletin, No. 185 (Nov., 1934). Cf. also R. P. Lane, "Review of Grape Breeding at the Georgia Experiment Station," *Harvester*, IX (1974), 19–24.

14. *Experiment Station Views* (Jan. 23, 1953).

15. R. P. Lane, "'Summit' Muscadine Grapes," *HortScience*, XII (Dec., 1977), 6. See also the Georgia Station's Research Report, No. 369 (Feb., 1978).

16. U.S. Department of Agriculture, Circular, No. 769 (Feb., 1948). For a discussion of how N. O. Booth's studies of pollen from *Euvitis* varieties paved the way for certain aspects of the muscadine researches, see N.Y. Dept. of Agriculture Experiment Station Bulletin, No. 224 (1902), pp. 291–302. For more recent crosses of *vinifera* with *rotundifolia*, see the bibliographies attached to H. Dermen et al., "Fertile Hybrids from a Cross of a Variety of *Vitis vinifera* with *V. rotundifolia*," *Journal of Heredity*, LXI (1970), 269–71; and John Einset and Charlotte Pratt, "Grapes," in *Advances in Fruit Breeding*, ed. Jules Janick and James N. Moore (West Lafayette, Indiana, 1975), pp. 130–53.

17. In Florida testing of muscadines was renewed in 1959 at Leesburg (C. F. Balestier and J. A. Mortensen, "Performance of Muscadine Grapes in Central Florida," *HortScience*, IV [Autumn, 1969], 252–53; and Mortensen, "Breeding Grapes for Central Florida," ibid., VI [Feb. 1971], 150–53). Of particular concern in Florida is resistance to Pierce's Disease. At Meridian, Mississippi, between 1941 and 1965 N. H. Loomis was active in the U.S. field station, the Magoon and Southland being two of the cultivars introduced there. Mississippi State Univer-

sity has more recently conducted excellent work in viticulture with the accomplishments of J. P. Overcash and in 1972 launched enological research in a new and well-equipped experimental winery on its campus. Southern grape breeders use this winery and the experimental enological laboratory of North Carolina State University for testing purposes (J. P. Overcash, *Bountiful, Chief and Southland Muscadine Varieties*, Mississippi Agricultural Experiment Station Bulletin, No. 995 [1967]; Overcash and B. J. Stojanovic, "Viticulture and Enology in Mississippi," *Mississippi Business Review*, XXXIX [May and July, 1977], 3–7. J. N. Moore reported on "Muscadine Variety Trials in Arkansas," *Proceedings of the Arkansas State Horticultural Society*, XC [1969], 62–66; and University of Arkansas Experiment Station Report, No. 200 [June, 1972]). In Georgia, R. P. Lane now shares the honors won by his eminent predecessor B. O. Fry, who since retirement from the university released several new cultivars through Ison's Nursery at Brooks, Georgia. In East Texas, at Overton, John A. Lipe, beginning in 1974, has been testing many varieties of muscadines with breeding materials furnished by R. P. Lane and W. B. Nesbitt. His first report was made by the Texas Agricultural Experiment Station in June, 1979; he found the scuppernong "highest in titratable acid." Among the distinguished grape researchers in North Carolina who carried on from the days of Carlos B. Williams are W. B. Nesbitt and V. H. Underwood, who have often been acting conjointly with Joe F. Brooks and Daniel E. Carroll, the last named a food scientist who has helped to revolutionize the manufacture of wines in the state.

18. Joe E. Brooks (Raleigh, N.C., 1978).
19. U.S. Dept. of Agriculture, *Muscadine Grapes: A Fruit for the South*, No. 2157, p. 13.
20. Dan C. Tucker, *North Carolina Vineyard Survey*, Statistical Bulletin, No. 133 (Raleigh, N.C., 1977).
21. Information from Ann Fussell, March 4, 1980.
22. Jack and Olivia Solomon, eds., *Cracklin' Bread and Asifidity* (University, Alabama, 1979), p. 14.

Index